# DECORATING WITHOUT FEAR

## A STEP-BY-STEP GUIDE TO CREATING THE HOME YOU LOVE

### SHARON HANBY-ROBIE

*Published by*
THOMAS NELSON
*Since 1798*

www.thomasnelson.com

Published in Nashville, Tennessee, by Thomas Nelson, Inc.

Thomas Nelson, Inc., titles may be purchased in bulk for educational, business, fundraising, or sales promotional use. For information, please e-mail SpecialMarkets@ThomasNelson.com.

Illustrations by Patty Minnick.

**Credits for chapter opener photographs:** *Chapter 1* Photographer: Patty Minnick; room courtesy of Steven L. Edris, Builder, Lancaster, Penn. *Chapter 2* Photographer: Lynn Noble; Interior Designer: Sharon Hanby-Robie. *Chapter 3* Photographer: Patty Minnick; room courtesy of Charter Homes and Neighborhoods, Lancaster, Penn. *Chapter 4* Photographer: Patty Minnick; room courtesy of Charter Homes and Neighborhoods, Lancaster, Penn. *Chapter 5* Photographer: Lynn Noble; Interior Designer: Sharon Hanby-Robie. *Chapter 6* Photographer: Patty Minnick; room courtesy of Charter Homes and Neighborhoods, Lancaster, Penn.

Text design by Bruce Gore.

**Library of Congress Cataloging-in-Publication Data**
Hanby-Robie, Sharon.
   Decorating without fear : a step-by-step guide to creating the home you love / Sharon Hanby-Robie.
      p. cm.
   Includes index.
   ISBN-13: 978-1-4016-0284-0
   ISBN-10: 1-4016-0284-3
   1. Interior decoration--Psychological aspects. I. Title.
   NK2113.H255 2007
   747--dc22
                                                                    2006039011

Printed in the United States of America
07 08 09 10 11 — 5 4 3 2 1

To all my wonderful clients who have helped
inspire me to create interior environments that delight;
to my smart and good-humored assistant, Patty;
to my dream-inspiring husband, Dave;
and to my Lord, Jesus

# C O N T E N T S

# ACKNOWLEDGMENTS

I am very grateful for all the clients who allowed me the pleasure of working with them and photographing their rooms for this book. I also want to acknowledge the builders who so graciously made their magnificent model homes available as well. A special thank-you goes to Charter Homes & Neighborhoods of Lancaster, Pennsylvania; Stephen L. Edris, builder, of Manheim, Pennsylvania; and Armstrong World Industries, ceilings and flooring divisions.

# CHAPTER 1

# Designing the Big Picture

- **STEP 1: PAY ATTENTION TO WHAT YOU LOVE**
- **STEP 2: DEFINE YOUR STYLE**
- **STEP 3: DEFINE THE ESSENTIALS AND ASSESS YOUR NEEDS**

**M**y goal as an interior designer is to help people discover their own personal style and give them the confidence to make choices that are logical for their families and lifestyles, yet beautifully self-expressive. Clients have told me that by doing this, I have given them the freedom to be themselves, and that after seeing their own creative ideas manifested, they have gained confidence in more than just decorating.

When I first meet with a new client, he or she is often focused on a specific item or room. But as a designer, I realize that making the most of any specific room requires understanding how the family functions throughout the house. Are there needs that are not being met, such as adequate study centers or entertainment areas, that could be accommodated in the room we are currently addressing?

As an interior designer, I approach each project as a one-of-a-kind situation, with the goal of getting into the hearts and minds of my clients to bring their needs and desires into reality. Establishing a strong relationship with my clients is necessary if I am to accomplish the goal of creating environments that are uniquely designed for the individuals residing there.

As you read, I will ask you the same prying questions that I would if you were sitting across the desk from me. It's a simple way for me to get to know you and your desires for your home. So let's get started!

# STEP 1: Pay Attention to What You Love

One of the most frequently asked questions that I hear when working with clients is, "Where do I begin?" My answer is, "Start with something you love." That may seem a bit too simple, but it is truly the best place to start. It could be a painting, a piece of fabric, a pillow, a vase, or even an antique relic that has been passed through the family. Of course, most people do pay attention to the latest trends and listen to the advice of what the current design guru might be saying. That's fine—it's nice to know what others think. But ultimately, the only opinion that should matter is your own. After all, this is your home—and it should be your fingerprints, your style, your colors, and your life that gets incorporated into it.

Creating a home that is uniquely designed for you and your family is a thoughtful process that requires commitment to the evolving plan.

Design is about your own way of seeing the world. Personal style includes everything that you touch and see. Your home should tell the story of your life. That means that completing your design will take a lifetime of building and believing in your own style. As you and your family grow and change, so too should your home develop to meet those changing needs. By simply incorporating possessions that you love and things that make you smile, the process will naturally evolve into an overall design that you find irresistible. As you continue to read, I want you to learn to trust your instincts and follow your heart.

Discovering your heart's desires is a process in itself. Have you ever walked into a home that was completely different from your own style and surprised yourself by responding to it in a very positive way? Perhaps it was a home that was for sale, a model home, or even a friend's home. Despite the fact that it was not what you considered "your style," you found it so appealing that you thought, "Why not try this for myself?" Perhaps it was a home filled with great American antiques. You loved it and suddenly wondered why you never considered such a style before.

If you have had an experience like this, I want you to reconstruct how you felt and discern what it was you might have been responding to. Did the home appeal to you because it was so graciously put together? Was it without the normal clutter and noise that daily life can bring? Was it simply the total atmosphere of calm and welcome that you found so appealing? Or was it the colors? Was there one specific trait, architectural feature, or piece of furniture that you remember finding particularly attractive?

Simply learning to be aware of your emotional response to environments is one of the important keys to identifying your own personal design style. Most people can more easily tell me what they don't like than what they do like. Part of the reason is that they are afraid to "commit" to something that they might have to live with for a very long time. Other times, it is a lack of confidence and an inability to trust or articulate their opinion and feelings.

**OPPOSITE (TOP)** A treasured family table can give a new home character and a connection to our lives. (Photographer: Patty Minnick; Interior Designer: Sharon Hanby-Robie)

**OPPOSITE (BOTTOM)** The simple necessities become works of art in this Shaker style kitchen. (Photographer: Patty Minnick; room courtesy of Steven L. Edris, Builder, Lancaster, Penn.)

**RIGHT** The richly hued colors accentuate the details and make this hand-painted armoire a very special feature in this room. (Photographer: Lori Stahl; Interior Designer: Sharon Hanby-Robie)

That's why, as an interior designer, I often feel more like a detective or a psychologist. When I first meet new clients, I put them through a series of probing questions. I will lead you through these questions in the pages ahead. This can be uncomfortable at first—but it's critical to the design process. I am careful to involve each person in the design process who is involved in the decision making. Husbands eventually appreciate being involved when they realize that I do honestly care about what they think and that I am also conscientious about budget. Money is one of the scarier aspects of design or decoration for many men. They assume that interior designers only know how to do things expensively. The reality is that as a professional I am more apt to know where, when, and how to save money than a nonprofessional. I have more than thirty years of experience working with families, their budgets, and their homes.

An easy way to help me further understand the likes and dislikes of clients is to have them go through magazines and pull ten to fifteen pages of rooms that they find appealing. I purposely ask them not to analyze the rooms. Instead, I want them to simply respond from their hearts and their emotions. This is something that I recommend you try. The key is limiting yourself to no more than fifteen pages. More pages simply clutter the results and overwhelm you. Less is best.

The analysis is something that I do together with clients so that I can help them delineate what specifically is most pleasing to them about each room. As you review your pages, you may find that what appeals to you about a space is the color, the accessories, one particular piece of furniture, or the overriding theme or atmosphere. This information is incredibly helpful in getting you to think outside your preconceived ideas about style. Rarely do most people have an opportunity to start from scratch when it comes to decorating—so this analysis of magazine pages will help you see how your rooms might look if you suddenly won a million dollars and could completely redesign your home.

If you are having difficulty deciding what it

**OPPOSITE**   The details of the country sink, tin punched cabinet doors, and cabinet hardware give this kitchen charm and function. (Photographer: Patty Minnick; room courtesy of Steven L. Edris, Builder, Lancaster, Penn.)

**BELOW**   The lighted cabinet gives this kitchen a special glow. (Photographer: Patty Minnick; room courtesy of Steven L. Edris, Builder, Lancaster, Penn.)

is you are attracted to in your sample pages, ask a friend to help you analyze the elements within each room. An outside perspective from a loving friend can be amazingly instructive. Be sure that you caution your friends not to respond with their personal reaction, but instead, to use their knowledge of you to help you uncover the things you love about each space.

## TRUST YOUR ARTISTIC IMPULSES

Have you ever purchased something that you found totally out of character for you? These items are another clue to discovering what you love. Perhaps you had no idea what possessed you to buy it and had no idea where you were going to put it when you got it home, but you simply loved it. I have items that I simply fell in love with even though they didn't seem to match my existing décor. I found many of my

throughout my home to a beautiful, formal lamp that mimics the beauty of coral. These things make my home more appealing to me. They calm me, they inspire me, and they allow me to remember the beauty of the sea and the refreshment that it brings me whenever I have the chance to spend time there. Learning to collect symbols of places that make you happy is a beautiful and simple way to make your home a comforting and inspiring place to be.

## IMAGINE YOUR IDEAL SPACE

What is your favorite room? Consider that it might not even be within your home, although I do hope it is. But sometimes our favorite space can be the place we naturally gravitate to when we need time alone—a favorite café or even a museum. Wherever your favorite room is, I want you to think about what it is that makes you want to be there. Is it an overstuffed comfy chair? Is it the quiet ambiance? Is it sun filled or dim? What color is it? The key here is to identify what it is that makes you want to be there.

When I ask clients to describe their favorite rooms, I am amazed at how their demeanor changes. They will smile or sigh as they begin to describe the image that is so clearly defined in

favorite treasures as I traveled. In most cases, I had no idea what I was going to do with the item when I got home, but I couldn't resist it.

These impulse gems are another glimpse into what your home might look like if you were able to fill it with things that you simply love. For example, in my heart, I live at the beach. The reality is that I live inland—nowhere near a beach. But I have filled my home with things that remind me of the beach, ranging from simple shells placed strategically their mind. They know these spaces. They love these spaces. My goal is simply to bring that same response to the rest of their home. If I can accomplish this, then they will love their homes.

Where do you love to vacation? Do you tend to go to the same place every time or do you like the adventure of finding new places to thrill and delight you? Is your favorite vacation spot quiet or energizing? What type of accommodations do you prefer? Are they rustic, formal, down-to-earth, or simply comforting? Vacations offer us the opportunity to rest and relax and to dream. Our idea of a dream vacation can give us insights to the type of environment we might design if we had the opportunity.

As you know, I love the beach. I also love to sail. I love the wind in my hair. As a result, building my screened-in porch was one of the best things I could have done for myself. When my goddaughter first saw it she said, "I feel like I am at the beach!" I was astounded but thrilled. My porch sits high above the lawn and is surrounded by trees and birds. When the sun sets, the view reminds me of when I set anchor for

the evening in a little harbor and watched the setting sun. I love it.

If you are adventurous and like to try new places every vacation, then I might suggest that we create spaces that allow you to change the feeling simply by changing a few key items or

accessories. Some people prefer consistency. For them, I create more finished spaces that change only when the light changes. Understanding our personalities and knowing our heart's desires gives us the ability to create spaces that we truly love and that, in a way, will create homes that "love us back" by eliciting specific emotional responses from us.

Whether we are aware of it or not, our environments affect our lives, even if only unconsciously. Restaurants, retailers, corporations, even churches are built to specifically evoke certain emotional and physical responses from us. So it only makes sense that our homes also be designed specifically to evoke responses from us that will enhance the quality of our lives.

Understanding that our homes are the only environment over which we have control makes the responsibility for creating loving, nurturing, comforting, and joyful spaces incredibly important. Eva Hagberg, a New York–based freelancer who writes about architecture, design, and culture, says in *Interior Design* magazine, "If individuals are delighted with their environment, you know everything's going to go well."

Your home offers an opportunity to create a world specifically designed for you and those you love. The atmosphere within will directly affect your attitude without. If your home creates havoc and anxiousness within your soul, then you can be sure that anxiety is exactly what you will carry to the outside world. The atmosphere we have and feel in our homes is what we teach those living there to expect. This is especially true for children, and positive or negative experiences in their childhood homes will affect them the rest of their lives. A place of tension and discord will teach our children to expect the same from the world. Poor design elements, such as clutter and illogical traffic flow, can create a negative attitude that might otherwise not exist.

Interior designer Kelly Wearstler says in *Circle Entrée* magazine, "Each room deserves dignity, respect and a healthy dose of laughter." I believe that you deserve dignity, respect, and a healthy dose of laughter, too. And I believe you should be able to find it within your own home. Take the time to discover your loves, your children's loves, and your mate's loves. Then fill your house with all this love and your home will become the best place on earth to live.

## NOW DO IT YOURSELF

Invest in a few home-decorating magazines. Tear out the pages that you find appealing, as I explained earlier. For each magazine picture, answer the following questions. Don't worry if you're not sure what "style" some of the rooms or furniture are. You'll learn more about styles in the next section.

- Is it formal or casual in style?

- Is it Country, Traditional, Contemporary, or an eclectic blend?

- Is there a specific chair or detail that appeals to you?

- What is its style—Chippendale, Neoclassic, Asian, French, and so forth?

- How is the room arranged?

- How many pictures are on the wall?

- Does the arrangement extend beyond the outer edges of the sofa?

- How high have pictures been hung?

- What are the overall shapes and sizes of accessories?

- Is there an abundance of smaller items or fewer larger items?

- What are the three main colors in the room?

- Are the colors pastel, bright, or gray in tone?

- How much pattern is in the space?

You now have a summary of personal design preferences that will help you begin your own home makeover.

**BELOW** A classic French bergère chair becomes a fashion statement when dressed in nontraditional fabrics and colors. (Photographer: Lynn Noble; Interior Designer: Sharon Hanby-Robie)

# STEP 2: Define Your Style

Now that you have an understanding of how to start your design plan around items you love, the next step in decorating is defining your style. What makes this a bit complicated is that in addition to specific furniture styles, such as English, Country French, American, Eighteenth Century, and so on, there is also your *attitude* style.

## RECOGNIZE YOUR ATTITUDE

Your attitude style has to do with how you want to live. Are you formal, casual, minimalist, or eclectic? For example, my style is a combination of Country French and Contemporary executed with a semiformal attitude. I love contemporary abstract art. I also love brightly colored paintings of flowers. Most of my floral paintings have a strong sense of color and shape that makes them work in harmony with the abstract paintings. My upholstery pieces are more traditional, but they are covered with fabrics that are a bit avant-garde. My French bergère chair has an amazing pink leather seat with a formal embroidered silk floral pattern of coral and pink on the back. Everything is comfortable and made for easy living. For me, it doesn't make sense to have a home that people are afraid to use. What elevates my attitude style from casual to semiformal are the Country French furnishings.

Casual is simply a relaxed, comfortable way of life: Casual living defines the type of place where you don't think twice about putting your feet up on the furniture. The fabrics will be durable and easy to maintain while the furniture arrangement will provide informal groupings that encourage conversation. It's the type

**ABOVE** The rich hues of this semiformal room capture the essence of Chippendale style in a room that evokes both sophistication and comfort. (Photographer: Lynn Noble; Interior Designer: Gail Dunn)

**OPPOSITE** A pencil post bed with its crisp lines, combined with a stylized rendering of an Amish family, is the perfect choice for this minimalist style bedroom. (Photographer: Patty Minnick; room courtesy of Steven L. Edris, Builder, Lancaster, Penn.)

of place where it's okay to do crafts on the dining room table.

Formal is a more gracious type of attitude. I often consider Southern style with its gentility and attention to detail as defining this category. I have a client who has beautiful, hand-carved mahogany furniture, new and antique, combined with rich mellow-colored fabrics. Her formal style blends items from today and the past. There is an abundance of accessories and mementos lovingly placed throughout. Graceful curves combined with a formal style of symmetrically arranged groupings add just the right amount of straightforwardness to this decorating attitude to make it work beautifully.

Minimalist style is for those who require simplicity in their lives. This simple style is about the integrity of the individual items that are carefully chosen for their distinctive lines. A minimalist is truly a person who believes that form follows function. A minimalist tends to like smoother, less complicated, sleek surfaces rather than ornately detailed ones. For example, a minimalist would not choose a hand-painted, multifaceted finish for a piece of furniture. Even color for a minimalist is defined. Minimalists love the crispness of black and white. They love gray tones paired with the spark of red. A few carefully chosen accessories define their decorating attitude and their design. Each item in the space makes a specific contribution to the overall scheme. There is nothing superfluous about their choices—nothing extra.

Eclectic style is a wonderful juxtaposition of the best of the first three decorating attitudes. It is playful, yet it has been carefully edited; it is the most flexible of attitudes. The hard part of being eclectic is not to end up with chaos. Learning to tame your attitude into a cohesive harmony is the key to making an eclectic attitude livable. Ultimately eclectic style is a mix of fun and function. I categorize Bohemian as a good example of eclectic style: You can make the combination of a high-styled gilded French mirror and a simple pine chest harmonious simply by choosing the right accessories.

## EMBRACE REGIONAL STYLE

The region in which we live affects our design style. I have several clients who have moved to Southern states for retirement. When they first settle in, most still have a Northern attitude. Many of them even choose to take some of their favorite furnishings with them rather than buy new. But within a few years,

they often feel their old Northern-influenced style begins to look out of place. The longer they live in a sunny, warm climate, the more their decorating style resembles the tropical environment in which they are living. The same is true for other regions. If you reside in a Southwestern region, eventually the characteristics of the area will be visible in your own style of decorating. That's okay. The key is developing your own characteristic style while allowing your new environment to influence your design decisions.

## ACKNOWLEDGE YOUR FRAMEWORK

Another important element to consider is your home itself. The architectural style of your home has a major impact in your design choices. The more specific and detailed the architectural style and features of your home, the more it will be reflected in your decorating style. For example, it would feel very disconnected to furnish a modern Frank Lloyd Wright–influenced home in the unrestrained, over-the-top Queen Anne Victorian style of decorating. Or can you imagine a Pennsylvania German style farmhouse furnished in formal Eighteenth Century Chippendale style decoration? Probably not. Historic homes of specific periods generally have such a strong sense of

character that makes them difficult to decorate in a style other than the one originally intended.

Most homes built since 1920 are less specific in regard to style. If they are Contemporary or Modern, their style is simple and easily identified. If they are neither, they fall into a catchall category defined as *Colonial Revival* style. This was a movement of designers between 1920 and 1950 who rejected the "modern" style of Frank Lloyd Wright. Many of the homes built during this period have multi-influenced characteristics and are not "pure" in style. However, they usually have at least one architectural element, such as the roof line or window placement, that we can use to characterize them as Queen Anne, Colonial, Cottage, or some other style. Nonetheless, in such houses no one consistent style

**RIGHT**  The best of all worlds comes together with an updated Traditional styling that includes doorway transoms, high ceilings, and hardwood floors. (Photographer: Patty Minnick; room courtesy of Charter Homes and Neighborhoods, Lancaster, Penn.)

**OPPOSITE**  The style of this room is traditional Williamsburg, but the attitude is all romance, from the hooked rug and needlepoint pillows to the Bullion fringed sofa skirt and silk taffeta draperies. (Photographer: Lori Stahl; Interior Designer: Sharon Hanby-Robie)

really prevails. In most cases, the architectural influence is not strong enough to force itself on your style. Ultimately, in these homes you can adopt the style that most appeals to you.

Traditional style is probably the most popular today, but also the most difficult to define. That's because it evokes design elements from so many time periods and cultures—from Country French to British Colonial or American Heritage. Traditional homes come in a variety of sizes, shapes, and interpretations. They might be two-story houses. They might be ranch houses. They are obviously not modern and that is the single characteristic that defines them as "traditional." They rarely have an architectural character that can be defined as one of the primary styles.

A Traditional style home may have architectural elements such as moldings and columns. Many of the newer homes being built today are what I consider "new" Traditional. They often include trayed ceilings (resembling an upside down tray), detailed crown molding, columns, wainscoting, and transoms over doorways. But their floor plans are more open than the Traditional homes of the past.

Other popular styles around America are Southwestern, French, and Mediterranean. Southwestern homes are generally one-story with flat stuccoed walls in light or earth tone colors. They are basically rectangular in plan with some variations. The roofs are usually a combination of flat and low-pitched gable with red tiles and exposed roof beams. These homes may have a

front porch, a vestibule, or portals with round arches and are generally unadorned. Windows are tall one-over-ones (the second-story window is placed directly over the first-story window), with picture windows also found in some homes.

The most distinctive characteristics of a *French* style home include the tall second-story windows, often arched at the top, that break through the cornice and rise above the eaves. This unusual window design is especially notice-

Frank Lloyd Wright

Queen Anne

Pennsylvania German Farmhouse

Chippendale

able on America's French Provincial homes. These homes were modeled after country manors in the French provinces. They are usually constructed of brick or stucco and are stately and formal. They have steep hipped roofs and a square, symmetrical shape with windows balanced on each side of the entrance. Mediterranean homes are typically multi-story and based on a rectangular floor plan;

**TOP (LEFT)**   Frank Lloyd Wright's "organic architecture" was a radical departure from the traditional architecture of his day, which was dominated by European styles that dated back hundreds of years. Wright's preoccupation with geometric forms and intersecting planes in his architecture led him to develop a similar style for furniture. The geometric designs of this oak chair with its dark wood finish are typical of Wright's style in designing chairs with a strong vertical and geometric emphasis. (Illustrator: Patty Minnick)

**TOP (RIGHT)**   Queen Anne style originated in England. It was the restrained English version of Rococo, which originated in France in the court of Louis XV. It is characterized by delicacy, restrained decoration, and curvilinear forms. These curving lines are best seen in this chair's cabriole legs, a new development of the period. Modeled after an animal's leg, the S-shaped cabriole leg gives furniture a more intimate, human quality than the massive turned legs of the William and Mary style. (Illustrator: Patty Minnick)

**BOTTOM (LEFT)**   Similar to armoires, kasten were brought to Pennsylvania by Dutch German immigrants. These large cupboards with double doors and sometimes drawers inside were used for storing clothes and linens. Today, they are perfect as large entertainment centers. (Illustrator: Patty Minnick)

**BOTTOM (RIGHT)**   The varied output of eighteenth-century London designer Thomas Chippendale included desks; mirror frames; hanging bookshelves; settees, with which he was especially successful; china cabinets and bookcases, frequently with fretted cornices and latticework glazed doors; and tables (such as the one shown here) with delicately fretted galleries and distinctive cluster-column legs of Gothic inspiration. (Illustrator: Patty Minnick)

they feature massive, symmetrical primary façades. Mediterranean Revival is generally characterized by stuccoed wall surfaces, flat or low-pitched terra cotta and tile roofs with arches, scrolled or tile-capped walls, and articulated door surrounds. Balconies and window grilles are common and are generally fabricated out of wrought iron or wood.

## DETERMINE YOUR FURNITURE STYLE

Once you have determined your decorating attitude and acknowledged the style of both your region and your home's architecture, the next step in decorating is choosing your furniture style. You also must decide whether you are a "purist" in style—meaning if you will follow to the letter the original historic definition of a particular period of time. A pure Eighteenth Century lover would never choose a fabric that was not consistent with the period, for example, and a purist would not introduce a contemporary painting into a historic space.

I have a client who is a purist in style. His home is an amazing Colonial Era log cabin home. Over the years, it has been updated to make it practical for today's living. But in doing so, every effort was made not to destroy the integrity of this historic property. All light switches are creatively hidden within the walls behind drop-down doors made of the same wood as the wall paneling. The lighting fixtures themselves were chosen and placed so that you do not see the source—only the light. When you walk into this home it is like walking back into history. It's fabulous. Of course, a few more compromises were made when it came to the kitchen and bathrooms, but even there, every effort was made to make the modern

conveniences harmonious within the context of the original time period of the home.

Awareness is the key to determining your furniture style. It's not so much a matter of why or

**ABOVE (LEFT)** The charm of this Cottage bedroom lies in its colors, patterns, details, and fresh, inviting approach. (Photographer: Lori Stahl; Interior Designer: Sharon Hanby-Robie)

**ABOVE (RIGHT)** This restored circa 1865 bed-and-breakfast started its life as a stagecoach shop. The formal parlor still retains its vintage style while continuing to accommodate guests from far and wide. (Photographer: Lori Stahl; Interior Designer: Sharon Hanby-Robie)

**OPPOSITE** The foyer of this Georgian Revival style home welcomes guests elegantly with its grand staircase and curving walls. Antiques and reproduction wall covering add charm to this classic atmosphere. (Photographer: Lori Stahl; Interior Designer: Sharon Hanby-Robie)

what—but more a matter of simply recognizing which styles most appeal to you. We usually know instinctively what makes us smile. We may not be able to articulate it or be able to identify it by name, but we do know it when we see it. Don't allow yourself to become confused by definitions—most any style can be adapted to fit your lifestyle. Interior design style today is less about rules and more about personalization and creating unique spaces that make sense for you and your family and the way you want to live. Allow this process to be an explorative journey of wonder and beauty. Allow your heart to guide you and you will not make a mistake.

I am not going to attempt to define all the styles of furniture over the history of the world. I have chosen simply to define the categories of styles that are most relevant for today's culture.

Recognize that although the styles themselves are explicit, many different factors affect the overall design. Today we are seeing Moroccan, Russian, Hispanic, and Island influences. Even "influences" have been influenced. There are British Island, French Island, and Caribbean Island styles appearing today. If you are romantic by nature, then that portion of your personality will show in your decorating style and attitude. Of course, each designer also adds his or her own flair and sense of style to make things even more interesting.

As you continue to explore, sometimes a clear and distinct style emerges as you examine various options. Other times, a fusion of styles becomes your defining vision. As you walk through showrooms and page through magazines, pay attention to the type of styles that you are drawn toward. Realize that sometimes couples choose opposite directions—and that's okay. Your goal will be to merge contrasting styles by choosing one as the most predominant and then letting the other style choice complement or add contrasting elements within the overall scheme.

To assist you in identifying your personal preferences, it will help for you to recognize the basic furniture styles. Traditional is the largest of all the style categories. It includes many styles, such as Country French and English; Formal Eighteenth Century French, English, Tuscan, or Italianate; Queen Anne; Chippendale; Art Deco; Victorian; and Neoclassic, among others. This style holds to the traditions of the past more than other designs. I find that my most conservative clients are usually traditionalist in style as well. Of all styles, Traditional is the most formal and often includes symmetrical floor plans. The furnishings have details such as

graceful curves and ornate carvings. Upholstery fabrics range from rich damasks and jacquards, to silks and chintzes. A Traditional style of decoration allows you to mix and match a variety of patterns, furniture styles, draperies, and carpet and flooring choices.

French furniture styles are diverse but have a common charm. From the rural country homes of France with their exposed rough-hewn beams and Country farm tables, to a formal Paris apartment with its gold-gilded chandelier and silk damask–covered settee, there is a distinct sense of style that cannot be ignored. The French style home includes multipaned windows and French doors and uses luxurious fabrics with lots of trim and cording to create the epitome of detail.

The French simply seem to know how to incorporate style with comfort in a unique way. A Country French chair displays the same exuberant detail in its carvings as a formal Louis XV—it is simply a matter of execution. While the formal French chair has been refined, the country chair is softer with less distinction. Yet both have a definite style that is clearly French.

Tuscan style has been incredibly popular over the past couple of years. I consider Tuscan the Italian version of Country French. Tuscan design is perfection in terms of style combined with enormous comfort and panache. Rich hues of red and gold permeate this rural style, just as those two colors enliven French décor. Overstuffed upholstery in lush yet sturdy fabrics are the hallmarks of fine Italian country living. Colorful handblown glass is the perfect accessory for a Tuscan room.

Neoclassicism (circa 1750–1820) was a new revival of classical antiquity styles. Architecture, furniture, and art began to reflect the characteristics of Roman and Greek art. Furniture reflected the rationalism of neoclassicism as it moved to straighter lines and less ornate décor. Neoclassic is a style that most people today shy away from because it can feel too formal. Yet I have a client whose home is completely Neoclassic but still inviting and comfortable. That's what is wonderful about design today—we have finally realized that comfort comes first. We adapt all styles to fit our comfort level.

Transitional includes such styles as Cottage, American Country, Tudor, and Craftsman/Bungalow. In fact, some might say that American style is pure transition. As a country we have had a difficult time defining our style. I worked on the renovation of a building from 1865 that included strong architectural elements and styles throughout the building from Georgian Revival to Colonial to Italianate. The client wanted to maintain true to period. The problem was choosing which style should be the most dominant.

Transitional style is influenced by the old Traditional style while making room for new style categories as well. Many of the new Traditional homes lend themselves to this style, which is more up-to-date than a pure Traditional style would be. Many of my clients embrace Transitional style because it allows them to use treasured family heirlooms or antiques alongside contemporary furnishings and art. It gives Traditional a current flair that translates perfectly for today's more relaxed style of living. When you imagine Transitional, think understated, relaxed, and inviting with a soft sophistication.

The fabrics used in Transitional spaces often include the richness of Traditional fabrics combined with interesting, more durable styles designed to handle real life. There is a lightness and level of freedom and flexibility that a purely Traditional home would not have. Think of a Country style home with its assemblage of natural elements and simple handcrafted furnishings that are pleasant and rich in textures and materials. Yet today this style has an up-to-date refinement that allows romantic, nautical, Shaker, and New England homes to easily adapt (transition) for our modern way of life.

The Contemporary/Modern category includes such styles as Arts and Crafts, Modern, Modern Asian, and High-Tech. Technically, anything new is considered Contemporary. Some people define *Contemporary* as "trendy." And others use the term *Contemporary* to define a softer version of modern. To keep things simple and avoid confusion, I prefer to use _Modern_ as the defining term for this category.

In the late nineteenth and early twentieth centuries designers such as Gustav Stickley, Charles Limbert, William Price, and others started the Arts and Crafts movement, which elevated the importance of craftsmanship over decoration. This new emphasis was more about quality in structure and less about artistic expression. Today, the Stickley style or brand of furniture continues to be popular. It is also a bit pricier because it adheres to the movement's original ethic of structural quality.

By the 1920s and 1930s a new expression was beginning to develop called the Bauhaus Art Movement, which strived to balance form, shape, color, and texture. After World War II we began to see sleek chrome designs that today we call _Retro_ style. This is the era that most people identify with Modern style. Modern style is simple and aesthetically pleasing. It is up-to-date with clean, crisp shapes. Modern furniture includes molded armless sofas, upholstered pieces with waves across the back, and steel- or fiberglass-framed seating. Today's modern upholstery seems to virtually mold to fit your

**BELOW** Even Retro style décor allows for a variety of textures that entice the senses. (Photo: MontesBurksCreative—Santa Fe)

body with the use of viscose elastic memory foam. NASA technology developed this foam that allows the weight and pressure of your body to be evenly distributed. If you push your hand into the surface of this foam, it will leave an impression for several seconds after you remove your hand. Ordinary foam regains its original shape immediately after your hand has been removed; it has no memory. This product cradles the body perfectly, providing amazing comfort. Modern design includes armrests that double as pillows for reading or watching television. The design focus is on simple forms artfully sculpted with bold lines. Modern design is considered to be fashion forward yet functional and efficient. It is perfect for someone who is a bit more daring and loves the look of a minimalist décor.

*High-Tech* style is simplicity and modernity at its best. It features stainless steel, chrome, concrete, and industrial architectural elements adapted for residential use. It is most popular for loft style living. But High-Tech design has also been embraced by those looking to create a home that removes the superfluous and focuses on simplicity. I saw one home in a desert setting that actually had a narrow trough cut into the concrete floors that were used for the entire interior of the home and extended outside to the patio. Within the 14-inch trough was a stream of water that ran from inside the home to the outdoors, providing natural hydration in what otherwise would have been a dry environment. It was simple, beautiful, and functional.

The kitchen is an area where High-Tech has managed to incorporate itself even in the most traditional of homes. Sleek metallic appliances with metal tubing for hanging kitchen tools and towels can work with almost any style.

Bathrooms too have benefited from the technology with glass block transparent walls. I used a glass block wall in the bathroom of a very traditional home recently. It was the perfect way to bring an abundance of natural light into the space without detracting from the rest of the architectural features of the home.

The *Southwestern* and *Mediterranean* categories are unique because they can be Traditional or Contemporary in style, yet they have characteristics and style unique to their origins. They often have a more rustic appearance—certainly less refined than a traditional Eighteenth Century style. Mediterranean and Southwestern interiors are similar in many ways. They both combine rugged materials, such as wood, iron, and honed stone. They both use brightly colored patterned fabrics, oversized furnishings, and natural materials such as leather and woven cotton. Southwestern style can be illustrated by a headboard that is upholstered in a kilim rug. A Mediterranean signature might be a panel screen made from cut sea glass.

Southwestern homes usually have stucco or adobe as their exterior finish material. Traditional renditions for a color scheme are often taken from nature, such as the color of a reddened sky at sunset. But we are certainly adapting the Southwestern home with new influences of color. Soft grays and greens combine to cre-

ate a desert oasis that calms the spirit. Many Southwestern homes are taking on a more minimalist interior style, making them more Contemporary than rustic. This refined statement complements a lifestyle of simplicity while maintaining a sense of origin.

Traditional *Mediterranean* style, whose

**OPPOSITE**   Sleekly sensational, this Modern style home adds texture to create a warm impression. (Photo: MontesBurksCreative —Santa Fe)

**BELOW**   The beauty of this Southwest home lies in its simplicity and focus on texture; it is the perfect desert sanctuary. (Photo: MontesBurksCreative—Santa Fe)

origins are in Italy, Greece, and Spain, also uses stucco for the exterior finish in which deep but narrow windows are placed and often flanked by slat-board shutters. The colors are vivid and rich to complement their seaside environment in tones that range from blues, greens, blacks, and whites to warm terra cotta and lavender with yellow combinations. Ceramic tile with mosaic designs is a mainstay in both Southwestern and Mediterranean homes. The tiles bring art and color to floors, backsplashes, and tabletops, creating a sense of centuries-old art and style.

Both Southwestern and Mediterranean style homes have large open living areas that simply invite nature and man to share the atmosphere. Walls are covered in layers of glaze, sand, and hand-rubbed texture that adds a quality that only time should be able to create. Today the similar Moroccan style is also influencing designers. With its burnished bronze urns, metal filigree light fixtures, and fireplace screens, complemented with bold red colors and teal colors patterned with gold filigree, it fits in with today's global influences and creates an atmosphere that I find encouraging and joyful. It makes me smile.

It is definitely worth the time and effort to discover your own unique style because it will please you for a lifetime. Don't give in to the lure of simply ordering a room full of furniture just to get the job done. It may fill the space, but it will not fill your heart.

**ABOVE**    From tabletop to floor, the textures in this Mediterranean style dining room encourage you to touch. (Photo: MontesBurksCreative—Santa Fe)

**OPPOSITE**    The Moroccan inlaid chest, hand-painted door, pottery, and tile floor all combine to create a highly sensory experience. (Photo: MontesBurksCreative—Santa Fe)

# STEP 3: Define the Essentials and Assess Your Needs

By now you realize that surrounding yourself with things you love is the key to making your home the peaceful retreat it should be. Hopefully, your personal style is beginning to emerge. We will continue to work on developing your personal style, but in the meantime, there are additional areas of exploration to consider. As you create a design plan, it is important that you understand the needs of your family. Whenever I bring up the topic of defining needs, I find that it usually initiates lively debate for many couples.

The reason is that men and women perceive *needs* differently. Many men define needs by comfort, masculinity, and technology. For them comfort is big, overstuffed seating, in rich, deep colors. The male gene apparently requires the latest, greatest, high-tech gizmo available. Men need a television, and not just any television; no, they need the monster, big-screen television, and they would prefer to operate the entire room via remote control from the comfort of their chair.

Women, on the other hand, usually begin the definition of our needs as something that looks good and makes us feel good. We need beauty in our lives. We recognize that we need comfort and functionality, but we are not willing to compromise on the design in order to accomplish it. In fact, when it comes to high-tech equipment, we want incredible sound from

## NOW DO IT YOURSELF

■ **If, after reading all these descriptions, you are feeling overwhelmed or confused, fear not.** As I said earlier, it really doesn't matter what your style is—it just needs to make you smile and make sense for your life. Once you identify what style makes you feel most at home, look specifically for design ideas and furniture that fit your style.

**ABOVE** A traditional oriental carpet is the anchor for this perfectly masculine home office with its deep rich woods and strong comfortable furnishings. (Photographer: Patty Minnick; Interior Designer: Sharon Hanby-Robie)

**OPPOSITE** This client's home office became a treasured space by incorporating meaningful mementos, her love of books, and a sense of comfort and serenity. (Photographer: Patty Minnick; Interior Designer: Sharon Hanby-Robie)

our music systems, but we would really prefer to not even see the actual components.

Understanding the difference between men's and women's needs makes the process easier to navigate. As a designer, I pride myself on being able to solve problems beautifully, and most of the time my clients feel that essential needs have been met. That's why it is so important for you to plan together as a couple or as a family and discuss *essentials* as well as dreams when it comes to defining your needs.

## EVALUATE YOUR FAMILY'S NEEDS

The process of assessment involves looking at your home as a whole in terms of functionality and identifying problem areas. But the process also requires that you assess each room individually as well. Many families perceive that one of their biggest issues is needing more space.

The reality is that most of us will fill whatever size space we are given. In fact, we would probably be much happier in a simpler, smaller space, if we could just bring ourselves to go through the process of elimination and pare down our belongings. I believe that most of us prefer quality over quantity. We just don't know how to accomplish that with what we have.

As I said earlier, even if you only want to make changes in one room, you still must do a comprehensive examination of your entire home to most effectively accomplish your goal. Let me give you an example. Recently I was working on the master bedroom for a client.

When I first saw the bedroom, I was astonished at the amount of furniture, clutter, and disorganization. As I began to look at the additional spaces on the second floor of their home, I realized that nearly every room had similar issues.

Most people would assume that there was a definite need for more space. But further examination revealed that other options existed. I discovered that the smallest room was being used both as a home office for the lady of the house, and as a homework center for her two teenage sons. You could barely walk into the space. Yet one of her sons had this wonderfully expansive bedroom that he used only for sleeping.

Before

Before

I suggested that we move her son into the small office/homework space and move the office/homework space into the large expansive room. Additionally, for the soon-to-be new office, I suggested they build two closets from floor to ceiling on either side of the door. One closet would house office equipment and supplies. The other could become the husband's clothes closet. To eliminate some of the furniture from the master bedroom, I had them move the husband's chest of drawers into the new office space as well. Because Dad often worked from home, we added two desks to the new office, one for her and one for him—basically dividing the space into one side for Mom and one side for Dad. Each of the children's bedrooms was large enough to accommodate desks for their homework.

Ultimately, with these changes, we were able to create enough space in the master bedroom closet, with a new organizational system, to easily accommodate the wife's clothing. We eliminated all the smaller, catchall baskets and

shelving from the room, which freed up more space so that we could actually add a writing desk to the master bedroom.

The decorating scheme was purposely designed to create a calm, clutter-free sanctuary. We removed the floral wallpaper, which only added to the atmosphere of clutter. A new hardwood floor and softly colored oriental carpet gave the room a new sense of airiness. We removed the slatted headboard and footboard and replaced them with a beautiful upholstered headboard, creating the illusion of more space by simply eliminating a footboard. Simple draperies and carefully chosen artwork were the final touches in this bedroom transformation. Just imagine how different the outcome might have been if I had not taken the time to completely evaluate the rest of their living spaces.

This family has called me several times since we finished this project to say that not only did I change their rooms, but I changed their lives. It's amazing the impact our environment has on our lives, even if we are not aware of it. When I first

After

After

**OPPOSITE (LEFT)** Before: Gaining perspective gives us the ability to make wiser decisions. This couple thought they needed more furniture in this bedroom to store all their clothing. But the problem was ultimately solved by rearranging the rest of the second floor and creating more useful and more beautiful spaces all around. (Photographer: Patty Minnick; Interior Designer: Sharon Hanby-Robie)

**OPPOSITE (RIGHT)** Before: This view of the same bedroom shows just how crowded spaces can get. A fresh perspective that only the camera could provide encouraged this family to tackle more than just the master bedroom. (Photographer: Patty Minnick; Interior Designer: Sharon Hanby-Robie)

**ABOVE (LEFT)** After: The transformation is breathtaking when we clear out the clutter and focus on creating a sanctuary. (Photographer: Patty Minnick; Interior Designer: Sharon Hanby-Robie)

**ABOVE (RIGHT)** After: Replacing the chest of drawers with a writing desk and beautiful artwork not only improved the view in the room, but gave this client an organized and inviting place to clear her mind by writing in her journal each evening before retiring. (Photographer: Patty Minnick; Interior Designer: Sharon Hanby-Robie)

met with the wife and mother of that family, she told me that she felt as if she were suffocating and stuck on an endless treadmill. Now she has not only gained a sense of control over her environment, but has discovered that she actually has more time since she no longer wastes precious moments searching for things that are buried in clutter. Our homes should meet our needs and be places of rest and renewal. Instead, too often we find ourselves overwhelmed, which drains our strength and energy.

My goal is to help you grasp the big picture of designing your entire living space while identifying the major and minor changes that can positively affect each room within your home. But to do so, you must be willing to carefully think about all the different types of activities that you expect to accomplish. Just as with this family, you can see that a myopic view might have led to a more organized office, but it would never have resulted in the major benefits that ultimately were realized by taking the process to the next level.

Just because you have always done something

a certain way within a specific room or space does not mean that you should or must continue to do so. Start by compiling a list of activities that you and your family currently are engaged in. Also consider those things you may have always wanted to do but haven't had the time, money, or opportunity. Perhaps you want to take piano lessons but can't figure out where a piano might fit, or are interested in weaving, pottery, or whatever. The goal here is simply to think about how you would change things if you could.

Perhaps you have a collection that has been boxed away for years because you can't figure

out where or how to display it. A couple who are clients of mine began collecting art many years ago—art is very important to them. I have specifically helped them create an environment within their home that allows them to showcase their collection. We have also planned for future acquisitions. Another client has a glass art collection, and a glass collection requires a completely unique set of criteria for exhibiting. Think about your loves, hopes, and dreams and begin to incorporate them into your home.

I often ask my clients to pretend that I have just given them a million dollars and the only

Before

place they can invest it is in their home. What would you do with your home if I gave you a million dollars? No, you cannot sell it and buy a new one. Start by thinking about your hobbies, your entertaining style, the phase or stage of life you are in, and the stage you expect to be in next. For example, if your children are young, how would you change your home when they become teenagers or when they leave home? What would your home and its rooms look like? Our homes should be designed so they can transform with the family's ever-changing needs. Embracing change gives you the freedom to dream about a better way of living.

As individuals in our society continue to live longer, it's not unusual for grandparents to become caregivers to their grandchildren while also caring for an elderly parent. This is the situation for one of my clients. My goal as a

**OPPOSITE** Before: The fireplace and flanking bookcases were dated and inconsistent in style with this client's tastes and collections. (Photographer: Patty Minnick; Interior Designer: Sharon Hanby-Robie)

**BELOW** After: Balance, proportion, and updated cabinets are the perfect complement for the glass art collection, which is enhanced by lighting from both above and below. (Photographer: Patty Minnick; Interior Designer: Sharon Hanby-Robie)

After

designer is to renovate her home into the beautiful place she has so longed for, while accommodating little ones running about as well as the needs of an elderly parent. Each decision we make regarding fabrics, flooring, or surfaces takes into consideration all the various concerns. She needs kid-friendly bathrooms that are also handicapped accessible. This client also loves to entertain. She has a large family and the dining room is still an important element for her. For others, who rarely use a dining room, we often find this to be valuable space for computers, homework, music, and crafting.

Another client of mine chose to completely eliminate the two-car garage. That large space became the much-needed family/play area for a family with young boys. Before making such a big decision, they thought long and hard about how long they thought they would continue to live in this home. They needed to make a long-term commitment that would ensure that the benefit outweighed the risk when it came time to sell later. We maintained the appearance of a garage from the outside. So eventually, if the new owners chose to do so, they could easily convert it back to a garage. When a neighbor of mine converted his garage to a family room, he took this idea to the next level by installing beautiful patio doors where the garage doors once were—a very attractive transformation.

## TAKE INVENTORY OF YOUR SPACE

As you assess your home, take an inventory of your square footage. Are there rooms or hallways where there is unused footage? So many homes have wasted valuable space in hallways. It is so easy to create traffic flow without the necessity for hallways. Hallways are also a great place to add storage and bookcases. Most people rarely miss the twelve to fifteen inches needed for such a structure.

How frequently are you using each space? Standard dining and living rooms that are rarely used should be readapted to make sense for the way you want to live. Are there some rooms or spaces that can perform double duty, like the room my clients converted into both an office and a dressing area for the husband? Can a guest room double as a craft room? Identify problem areas within each space. For example, are you struggling to arrange your family room to accommodate seating and television viewing for everyone? If so, think about how a few simple changes to the overall floor plan of your home might improve the situation.

If you don't have a blueprint of your home, make a sketch of your entire first floor and another of your second floor. Evaluate each floor individually. Where do you spend most of your time? In most cases, families gather in the kitchen and family room. Are those spaces inviting? Are they large enough for everyone to be comfortable, or are you crammed together in an inhospitable room that could completely be transformed by simply moving a wall two feet out? Would a larger, more informal eating area with a dining table designed to accommodate homework and crafts make more sense than maintaining an eat-in kitchen and a dining room? Imagine how different these spaces might be by simply adding larger windows. Would removing a small section of wall between your dining room and kitchen create a more accommodating traffic flow?

Realize that with good planning, remodeling or refurbishing your spaces can be accomplished in stages. Changes can take place one step at a time, over an extended period of time. This gives you the opportunity to live with each new change and carefully plan your next idea without the overwhelming pressure to do it all at once. An effortless way to experience new ideas is simply to move your furniture and activities within those zones where you are considering changes.

Changes within our homes can easily lead to lifestyle changes that can affect our intimate relationships with family as well as our extended relationships with friends and community. As we move toward being a culture that is more community oriented, entertaining in our homes has again become an important element of enriched living. Entertaining styles greatly affect how we situate and use the spaces of our

**BELOW**  This children's room swings with a funky theme. The giant record makes a terrific headboard while adding a unique character. (Photographer: Patty Minnick; room courtesy of Charter Homes and Neighborhoods, Lancaster, Penn.)

home. I seem to entertain at two extremes—either we have a few friends for dinner or we invite the entire cast and crew from the local theater. Having an open floor plan that easily accommodates movement throughout makes sense for our way of life.

With many people now working from home, the idea of a truly functional home office is hardly a luxury. Even if you don't telecommute, everyone needs a place to manage finances and pay bills. As you analyze the floor plan of your home, consider where a home office would be most appropriate. Would a home office make sense on the first floor of your home? Or would noise and general interruptions from family be too invasive?

Many of my clients need two home offices. That's the case for my husband and me. Because we both require quiet for our work, we chose to place our offices as far from one another as possible, so if either of us is engaged in a phone call we don't disturb each other. Generally, experts would say that women prefer smaller, more intimate spaces for their offices. We generally like to fill our spaces with music and books and lots of sunshine. Men prefer larger, manlier spaces, and because they often have a television in their office, light shining in on it is not ideal.

Growing children have needs too, especially when it comes to keeping order. We'll discuss organization in detail in Chapter 2. For now, just make sure that you take into consideration the activities of your children as you are assessing needs. A study by the American Society of Interior Designers found that regardless of age, adults and children alike expressed two identical needs: Both groups want a place to come together as a family, and both need a place to retreat to for quiet time. Children in particular

benefit from a "calming down" or "meditative" place where they can go when they are feeling wound up, according to Barton Goldsmith, PhD, author of *Emotional Fitness for Couples,* and this can be good for parents as well.

Our homes are likely the only environments over which we have full control. Within them we have the power to create safe, nurturing, comfortable spaces where we can all thrive, physically, spiritually, and emotionally. Our homes can and should positively influence our lives. It's all a matter of design. As William Morris (1834–96), the British craftsman, designer, writer, typographer, and socialist said at an address delivered before the Trades' Guild of Learning, "To give people pleasure in the things they use, that is one great office of decoration; to give people pleasure in the things they make, that is the other use of it."

## NOW DO IT YOURSELF

■ **Write a list of activities you do or want to do in your home.** What equipment or supplies will you need for these activities? If you want to take up weaving, you will need a lot of open space for a loom and yarn storage. If music is on your agenda, perhaps you need to consider creating a soundproof area.

■ **Make a list of empty, unused spaces throughout your house.** Clearing out clutter and unused items from valuable square footage can give you the extra room you need. How often do you really use your guest room? If it's only a few times a year, then convert it to a more usable space.

■ **On a drawing of your floor plan, create new areas for focused activities.** Sometimes it takes seeing the possibilities in black and white to motivate us to make our dreams become reality. By drawing plans for your dreams, you create a contract with yourself to move forward.

# Live with What You Love and Get Rid of the Rest

- **STEP 1: THE KITCHEN—THE HEART OF THE HOME**
- **STEP 2: A ROOM FOR LIVING**
- **STEP 3: A BEDROOM SANCTUARY**
- **STEP 4: THE BATH—YOUR PERSONAL BEST BATHING BEAUTY**
- **STEP 5: THE BEAUTY OF A HOME OFFICE**
- **STEP 6: LAUNDRY ROOMS AND MUDROOMS**

**A**t first, the idea of addressing clutter may not seem like a very romantic or even a relevant concept when it comes to interior decorating or design. But after working with families for over thirty years, I know that nearly everyone has at least one area within their home that could use a little organizational help. It's amazing what happens to a home when we get rid of clutter and thin out our possessions to a few simple but meaningful choices. Even if you do not consider yourself a minimalist and prefer layers of collections and mementos, there is an art to such adornment that requires a bit of editing to create the balance and harmony necessary.

When I work with clients, I usually work through the process of decluttering one room at a time. So this is the approach I will use here: I will ask you to analyze how each room is used and to consider changes or new visions for each space. As we walk through your home on this journey together, I want to engage you in the art of design and decoration as well. My goal for this chapter is to help you clean out your spaces from the daily clutter to find the freedom for self-expression and revitalization for your home.

# STEP 1: The Kitchen— The Heart of the Home

Designing a kitchen, whether big or small, should be a labor of love. Even experts find it challenging to create a room that meets the needs of everyone within the family. My mom is a kitchen and bath designer, and she agrees that no matter how inviting the rest of your home, the kitchen is where everyone seems to congregate. The cooking area has been the center of activity since the discovery of fire. We expect a lot of use from our kitchens. It's not just a room for cooking, but for entertaining and working as well. Music and media centers, computers and high-tech appliances are all expected to fit into a space that is also visually appealing.

Kitchens also seem to be the place to drop nearly everything that you carry into the house from work, school, or play. Whatever is in your hands usually ends up somewhere in the kitchen, along with the mail, newspapers, and packages. Consequently, kitchens are the most challenging spaces to keep clean and organized.

I want you to think back to when you first moved into your kitchen. You know, the day when everything was finally unpacked and put away. It started out neat and organized. Then life happened, and before you knew it you owned three containers of oregano because you couldn't find the first or second one that you purchased. A cluttered kitchen can be overwhelming. If like in my house, the kitchen is the first space you see when you walk into your home, it can agitate your mood before you even get your coat hung. I often encounter cluttered countertops, overpacked cupboards, and papers littering the table in the kitchens of my clients. Add to that a refrigerator completely covered in magnets, notes, calendars, recipes, and children's art while the bulletin board nearly falls to the floor from the weight of its burden.

## THROW SOMETHING AWAY

Decluttering is always about a simple process of elimination. I want you to start with a garbage bag and two boxes. One box will be marked for items that actually belong somewhere in the kitchen and the other for things that need to find a new home in another room. Then add a box for each member of the family.

**LEFT**  The tribal rugs in the kitchen not only help create a cohesive color scheme throughout the open floor plan, but bring in warmth to make the spaces cozy and inviting. (Photographer: Patty Minnick; Interior Designer: Sharon Hanby-Robie)

**BELOW**  Fresh, clean, and sophisticated details give this kitchen a timeless appeal. (Photographer: Patty Minnick; room courtesy of Charter Homes and Neighborhoods, Lancaster, Penn.)

Begin clearing your countertops by making quick decisions: Old unread newspapers—toss into the garbage bag for recycling. When it comes to magazines and catalogs, be realistic about your time. If you truly love the magazine and feel as though you get pleasure and worthwhile information from it, place it in your box; otherwise toss it out. Continue and be ruthless. The idea is to end up with less, not simply with items to move elsewhere.

Once you have tackled all the surfaces within the kitchen, move onto cabinets and drawers. A cabinet or drawer is a major project, but each space can be handled within fifteen minutes. Don't become overwhelmed and give up. The best approach here is an organized one. For example, one day I tackled all the glassware and cups/mugs/travel mugs. I was astonished at how many travel mugs we own—and there are only two of us! I ended up packing away or throwing away nearly half of what was in my kitchen just in this one category. Now when I open the cupboard door I don't have to worry about being hit by an avalanche of cups!

Once you have decluttered your kitchen, it's time to reorganize it. One of the simplest ways to approach the process of organization is to think in terms of workstations. Take a critical

look at your kitchen layout. Sometimes moving a single appliance can make a world of difference. Recently, one client removed the wall oven that impeded traffic each time it was open. She then replaced the cooktop stove with a full range and oven. The opening created from the old wall oven now holds the microwave. These few simple moves made their kitchen functional and traffic friendly.

Now think about where you use certain items in your kitchen. For example, if you use your microwave a lot, place all your microwave-able bowls, plates, and other containers near the microwave. Organize pots and pans in close

vicinity to the stove. Deep drawers are the ideal place for keeping such items.

Dishes, glasses, and cups should be closest to the dishwasher and the refrigerator, if possible, to make using them and putting them away a

**OPPOSITE** Even a small kitchen can be beautifully functional and inviting. This updated Country kitchen welcomes cooks and friends alike. (Photographer: Patty Minnick; room courtesy of Charter Homes and Neighborhoods, Lancaster, Penn.)

**ABOVE** Deep, dark wood cabinets complement granite countertops and rich mahogany flooring—the ultimate in sophistication. (Photographer: Patty Minnick; room courtesy of Charter Homes and Neighborhoods, Lancaster, Penn.)

simple move. Store all coffee paraphernalia together to make it easier to start your morning. If you simply think about your activities within the kitchen and organize accordingly, it will function much easier.

If you are like me, you probably have a multitude of plastic storage containers. Like clothes hangers, containers seem to multiply behind closed doors. Let me suggest that you go through and toss out every stained, half-melted, and lidless one in the bunch. That alone should free up at least a shelf in your cupboard. Another category that seems to continue to grow is cooking and baking utensils—spatulas, ladles, mixing spoons, serving spoons and forks, salad servers, measuring spoons, and so on. It's easy to collect an abundance of little corn holders, carving knives, apple cutters, garlic presses, wine cork pullers, and other specialized items that can clog your kitchen drawers. Simply trying to locate the meat thermometer can take five minutes—by which time the meat is burnt! These seldom-used tools also need editing. If you only use them once or twice a year, there's no point in their taking up valuable space. At least put them all in one of the more out-of-the-way drawers. Keep tools that you use every day in easy reach of the area where you use them.

Of course, no kitchen would be complete without a junk drawer or two. The goal here is to toss out anything that cannot be identified. Start by dumping the entire contents out on the table and begin sorting. I found that forcing myself to use drawer organizers or trays in my junk drawer eliminated the possibility of putting many of those items back in—they just wouldn't fit in the compartments—which was a good thing. Drawer dividers are perfect for organizing small items such as paper clips, rubber bands, and twist ties. They also work great for pens, letter openers, scissors, and coupons.

Continue the purging process by moving seldom-used appliances, such as blenders, mixers, bread makers, and so on, to a remote location. For my mom, we added storage in the garage to house those things she uses only seasonally.

In an ideal world we would each have a pantry the size of a walk-in closet. But you don't have to own the world's largest pantry to get it organized. Simply choose a space-saving system of shelving that works best for you. Most pantries are equipped with deep shelving designed to hold a lot of food. But if items get buried deep in the recess of the shelf, limiting access and visibility, you probably won't find them when you need them. If at all possible, I recommend using narrower shelving or tiered shelving instead.

The best way to organize pantry items is by category, keeping nonfood items separate from food items. Don't forget about the pantry door. It can be fitted with an over-the-door rack to create valuable space for canned goods, paper goods, and spices. Pullout bins are also perfect for storing in a pantry. A deep drawer is another helpful feature that can be added to the bottom of the pantry. It's perfect for storing little-used appliances, bags of pet food, and so on.

If you don't have a pantry, look for wall spaces that can be converted for storage. For one client we discovered the ideal place was the walls on either side of the staircase leading to the basement. The wall was recessed from the rail area by 5 inches. We purchased narrow basket-style wire mesh shelving in varying sizes and filled the space with them. She was able to fit all

**ABOVE** Distinctively stylish, these glass door kitchen cabinets are perfect for those who run a neat ship. They're fresh and clean, and it's so easy to find exactly what you need. (Photographer: Lynn Noble; Interior Designer: Gail Dunn)

the pet food, teas, soup cans, spices and other baking ingredients, and paper goods into them.

Organization is only as good as your ability to maintain it. So think practically as well as decoratively as you consider your organizational skills and kitchen habits. If you love to keep everything looking tidy, then storing plates and other essentials out in the open may be a perfect option for you. If on the other hand, putting away groceries quickly and hiding clutter is more your style, than admit it and organize accordingly behind closed cupboard doors.

Once you've accomplished the goal of decluttering and reorganizing, step back and enjoy the peaceful view. Clutter creates chaos, and chaos creates stress. Your kitchen is now stress free. As author and organizing expert Peter Walsh says, being organized helps you live a richer life. I know that he is correct. Every time I take clients through this process of organizing their clutter, they feel relieved at the sense of control they have gained. They enjoy their spaces again instead of being overwhelmed by them. When rooms have breathing room, so too does your life.

## EXAMINE THE TRAFFIC FLOW

Now it's time to examine how well your kitchen floor plan is functioning. Unless you happen to have a new kitchen, you are probably

dealing with a layout that was designed for another time and place, which is totally irrelevant to the way you want to live. But a few simple changes can make a world of difference. One client's refrigerator blocked the entry from the back door every time she opened it. She finally removed the wall between the kitchen and dining room to create more room and to eliminate the traffic logjam.

Moving your kitchen table and other furnishings around may allow you to create a cozy niche. For a client living in a small town house, we made the most of her space by building a cushioned banquet in a small corner and adding a roomy table. Above the banquet we added tall shelves to the ceiling. They are perfect for neatly and beau-

tifully housing not only her cookbooks but other books, electronics, CDs, and collectables.

All kitchens have common requirements. But each family has unique needs. The key to a successfully designed kitchen is assessing your family's specific needs. Do you need a homework center? Are there hobbies that require special equipment? For example, one of my clients loves to bake pies, so when reworking his kitchen we focused on creating space so he could easily enjoy his hobby. Perhaps you enjoy candy making or like to make your own pasta. When you think about how you want to use your kitchen, you need to ask yourself a series of questions that will prompt ideas and changes to make your kitchen more accommodating to your ideal life.

Do you want a television in your kitchen, or a computer? Do you have collections you would like to display in your kitchen? Do you entertain? If so, how often and for how many people? Perhaps you have special dinnerware that you use for entertaining. If so, a second dishwasher that doubles as storage for that dinnerware might make sense for you. Will your children be hanging out in the kitchen? If so, incorporate space for them. One expert recommended giving children their own cabinet space in the kitchen for toys, games, and craft items. I also think it is an excellent idea to give young children a small table with chairs their own size, if you have the room.

How many cooks are there in your home? Do you cook together or take turns? The answer to this question will certainly affect how you lay out your kitchen. For two cooks in the kitchen I would plan for 42 inches of space between parallel countertops at workstations. A two-chef kitchen also calls for doubling up on other items such as sinks and ovens.

Your personal cooking style will also affect

**OPPOSITE** This kitchen is designed for entertaining, with plenty of room for guests to keep you company while you cook. The stainless steel appliances fit perfectly in this Transitional décor. (Photographer: Patty Minnick; room courtesy of Charter Homes and Neighborhoods, Lancaster, Penn.)

**BELOW** It's amazing how a few accessories can add so much charm and character to a kitchen. Who can resist the vaulted ceiling and the aged wood floor? This kitchen is simply inviting. (Photographer: Lynn Noble; Interior Designer: Gail Dunn)

how you arrange your kitchen. I need a little calm and some space when I am preparing dinner. For me, a separation between the cooking area and the dining and entertaining area is helpful. I created a semi-island by extending the lower cabinets out at an angle between the two areas. It gave me additional storage and countertop space but more importantly, it gave me the space I need for food preparation without feeling crowded.

No man—or woman—need be without an island. A kitchen island can give you more than simple counter space—it can give you flexibility and added storage as well as a place for family and friends to gather around. A curved island is a great way to encourage conversation. Some of the smallest kitchens can accommodate a "moveable" or temporary island. An island with casters can be pulled around as tasks dictate. Even a fold-up cart that can be stored away can give you the additional space you need when baking or entertaining. The best part of a kitchen island is the personality that it brings to the room.

A hard-working island can be built to match your cabinets, but it is also the perfect place to unleash your creativity. My friend Jan found an old, worn, rustic butcher-block table that is the perfect complement to her country kitchen. If you love modern, why not try a stainless steel worktable as an island? Don't be afraid to add color and texture with an island. Even if the rest of your cabinets are stained, a painted island can bring your kitchen to life with personality. If you have perfectly painted cabinets, then try a worn painted patina in a different color for your island. This is an easy and effective way to express your personality.

## CREATE A FUNCTIONAL AND BEAUTIFUL SPACE

Ultimately your kitchen should be as inviting as it is functional. After all, it is the hardest-working and most-often-used room in the house. Because you will spend so much time in this room, it should attract you with little details that enhance the entire room. The best ideas for your kitchen will come from your own answers to what makes you happy while preparing meals.

How do you want your kitchen to feel? I love an open airy kitchen with lots of light. I love the clean, fresh feel of white cabinetry infused with color from artwork, floral arrangements, and other accessories. I walk a fine line between functional, formal, and fun. I call it elegant with a sense of surprise. My Country French carved

**OPPOSITE**   This Country French bench makes the transition from my living room to kitchen perfect. The coral embroidered pillows add my signature of a seashore theme beautifully. (Photographer: Lynn Noble; Interior Designer: Sharon Hanby-Robie)

**BELOW**   My kitchen makes me smile with my collection of birdhouses and enormous bird sculptures—the brilliant colors help make my mornings bright. (Photographer: Lynn Noble; Interior Designer: Sharon Hanby-Robie)

bench is filled with colorful pillows, while my collection of birdhouses and enormous bird sculptures add to the fun with even more brilliant color. A farm table surrounded by red lacquered chairs invites guests to sit and enjoy the surroundings in comfort.

Special details make your kitchen personal, but that doesn't necessarily translate to expensive. A display of sentimental heirlooms can make your kitchen unique and significant. A set of antique dishes or a collection of teacups that you treasure can become the inspiration for your entire decorating scheme if properly displayed. Fabrics can add charm, make a style statement, and add softening to the kitchen's otherwise hard-surfaced environment. Seat cushions, valances, crisp curtains, and table linens can bring your own sense of style and comfort while helping to absorb sound.

For me, table linens are one of the easiest ways to change the mood in my kitchen. I have a collection of linens that range from 1950s style to elegant hand-embroidered ones. I transform my kitchen with each season simply by changing the table linens. Sometimes changing color and adding more lighting can be just the lift your kitchen needs. (I'll be discussing the specifics of color and lighting in Chapters 3 and 5.) As the heart of the home, let your kitchen reflect your personality for gathering, cooking, and simply living.

## NOW DO IT YOURSELF

■ **Make three lists: the essentials, the added extras, and the unnecessary.** (Just because everyone else has a toaster oven doesn't mean you need or want one.) Consider this list for a few months, editing as needed. When you are sure it is complete, begin to incorporate those changes.

■ **Do you need a place to keep cookbooks near at hand?** Consider having a shelf built near your baking center. If you lack room in your kitchen, keep only the books you use regularly, and store the additional cookbooks in another room. Keep your kitchen shelves free for what you use daily. I chose to build in a bookcase with storage below in the hall at the back door entry. In a space that is only 36 inches wide and 18 inches deep, I have gained an amazing amount of organized storage.

■ **Organize a place in your kitchen for cutting and chopping foods.** This might be near your sink, where the fruits, vegetables, and cutting board can be easily rinsed after cutting. Chopping tools and knives can be kept in the nearest drawer. Magnetic strips mounted on the wall are also ideal for keeping knives within reach and away from small children.

■ **Create a designated breakfast station to make your morning less chaotic.** Keep cereal and cereal bowls, coffee, tea, mugs, and spoons together to make it easy for everyone to help themselves.

■ **If you have pets, designate an out-of-the-way area for feeding them to avoid knocking over water bowls or slipping on pet food.** You need only about 2 square feet of floor area for food and water bowls. If you are remodeling, leave an open area beneath a cabinet that is 18 to 24 inches high.

■ **Wallpaper or paint on your kitchen walls can infuse your kitchen with personality.** Add an area rug, seat cushions, table linens, and accessories that speak your style to transform your kitchen from practical to inspirational.

# STEP 2: A Room for Living

I love the way our living and family rooms have become the center of activity. We read, watch television, do homework, play games, wrestle with the dog, do paperwork, pursue hobbies, listen to music, and, of course, spend time with family and friends in our living and family rooms. Every activity has a corresponding set of equipment and items, and the more living we pack into these rooms the harder it is to keep them clutter-free and organized.

The good news is that you are not alone in the challenge to make living areas user-friendly and attractive. Although our specific activities may differ, we all fight the same battle of balancing workspace supplies with restful places to retreat. We want to enjoy living and using our living rooms, but we also have an innate desire to enjoy the view.

When we first furnished these spaces they were probably organized. But over time clutter happened. The problem is that disorganized clusters of papers and piles of supplies can accumulate so gradually that we don't even notice how disarrayed the room has become. The chaos of clutter certainly affects us, even if it's on a subconscious level, but often we simply stop seeing it. One client recently admitted that she had learned to walk a new path to her living room because the Christmas ornament boxes were still sitting in the middle of the hallway. For four months she has walked around them, which just proves how adaptable we are. For all intents and purposes, she no longer even sees the boxes.

To help clients gain control over the clutter and storage issues in their homes, I needed to find a way to help them see the reality of their situations. I have found a helpful technique that allows my clients to have the same perspective I have when I first enter their home. I take a picture. Yes, a simple photograph reveals the truth of what we often choose to no longer acknowledge. Whenever I use this little trick with my clients, they are shocked. It's amazing what the camera shows. I suggest you grab your camera and take a candid walk through your home—no prepping allowed. Take a picture from four different perspectives of the room. Then examine the photos.

Sometimes what becomes apparent is how out of proportion accessories, wall art, or even furniture is for the space. Other times, the photos show that clutter is out of control. Snapshots reveal obvious items that should be picked up daily and put away. In the midst of our busy lives, we let things go, expecting to deal with them later—but "later" eventually becomes "never," and before we realize it, many misplaced items take up permanent residence in our living room. The photographs usually inspire my clients to address the issues that need immediate attention.

**BELOW** Everyone needs a place to relax and find a bit of quiet. This sitting room makes it easy to let your mind take a little time off and simply unwind. (Photographer: Patty Minnick; room courtesy of Charter Homes and Neighborhoods, Lancaster, Penn.)

But if you need further motivation, simply think about the benefits of getting organized. With less stuff in the family or living room, you will have more space for family and friends. If your room looks neater, you will be more inclined to welcome people who drop in without warning. And perhaps your home will even become the social gathering place. You may also find your room so inviting that you want to spend time there simply reading or relaxing. One client said after a major organization plan was implemented, "I just want to go in there and read."

The most motivating factor for taking control of clutter and storage is that it will reduce the amount of time needed for cleaning. According to Kathy Paauw, Principal of Paauwerfully Organized, cleaning professionals agree that simply getting rid of clutter will reduce the time needed to clean by 40 percent.

From my bag of tricks, here comes trick number two: Remove everything from your room that you can carry. That's right, everything that you can carry; that includes lamps, artwork, books, CDs, ottomans, small tables, whatever. The only things left should be the largest pieces of furniture and of course, those items that are built in. Now here's the most important part of the magic—you are only allowed to bring back in 50 percent of what you removed. Trust me, by the time you have put half of it back, you will begin to wonder how it all managed to be in there in the first place.

As you are pondering which half will be returned to the room, make note of the types of things that you want to keep there. If you own a lot of books and CDs, as I do, then I might suggest that you build in bookshelves. This is one of the simplest and most efficient ways to use vertical space. You only need 12 to 20 inches of depth. I recommend building the shelving all the way to the ceiling. You can use the higher shelves for those books that you seldom access.

**OPPOSITE**  The warmth of gold and red makes this room incredibly cozy while the choice of leather makes the seating especially durable. This is the kind of room you don't hesitate to put your feet up in. (Photographer: Patty Minnick; room courtesy of Charter Homes and Neighborhoods, Lancaster, Penn.)

**BELOW**  Your home should accommodate your passions. This family loves books, so they are center stage with plenty of room to grow. (Photographer: Patty Minnick; room courtesy of Steven L. Edris, Builder, Lancaster, Penn.)

If you add doors to the upper shelving you can hide seasonal decorations there as well. With drawers or doors added to the lower section, you instantly gain storage for CDs, games, hobby supplies, even a throw or two for a cold winter evening. Often I build shelving behind or on either side of the sofa. Those few inches usually aren't missed in the living space and the abundance of storage gained is amazing.

## KEEP LIVING ROOMS PRACTICAL AND PURPOSEFUL

Choose carefully those items you want to return to the room, recognizing that this does not have to be an emotionally wrenching experience. I won't ask you to throw out your great grandfather's hand-painted desk. I may ask you to move it, but I won't tell you to use it as firewood. All of us keep things because they have sentimental value. You may be attached to your

favorite album from the seventies, but you probably haven't listened to it since the eighties. Pack it up. If you can't bring yourself to give it away or toss it out, then store it—just get it and other unused items out of the living room.

Even heirlooms often outlive their purpose. One client had a particularly old family chair in her family room. It was so fragile that she was afraid to sit on it, even though they desperately needed all the seating they could manage. Finally, she was willing to compromise when I convinced her that it made far more sense for this chair to become a decorative accessory in a hallway rather than take up valuable seating space in the family room. Family heirlooms are fine, as long as they make sense for the way you want to live and are not simply taking up valu-

able space that prevents you from having more functional furnishings.

The goal in creating storage for this most visible of spaces should be to make it as beautiful as possible, easy to access, and consistent with your décor style. When choosing furnishings and accessory items, look for hidden storage. Large-scale storage cocktail ottomans are one of my favorite ideas because they provide a place for game playing, eating pizza, storage, and a place to put your feet up. Trunks, armoires, and even end tables with storage can add much needed space to help keep you organized. Simply zone them to store specific items. These dual-purpose pieces of furniture are especially helpful in small spaces. For a client who lives in a Manhattan apartment, we chose a cocktail table whose top lifted and moved forward, making it usable as a desk or a dining table. In addition, it contained two large file-sized drawers. It was the perfect selection for her small space.

Another way to control clutter in these spaces is to prevent it from getting there in the first place. One client complained that every night her husband dropped his backpack and shoes in the living room. It had turned into the daily rift between them. By discussing it together, they were able to develop a simple solution by adding a hook and cubby for his belongings right at the entry door. They found a way to compromise by providing an alternative that was as easy as dropping his belongings in the living room. The new habit took only a few weeks to master and it made everyone happier.

Take time to think about your family's traffic patterns and the types of things they carry with them as they enter and leave the house. Then create "dropping places" near their point of entry. This can keep a lot of clutter in an organized place. Many times I find that living/family rooms also have a guest coat closet nearby. This is an easy place to add a few drawers or shelves to gain additional space for storage.

In family rooms creative storage for big electronics can either make a significant design statement or can be designed to fit inconspicuously into the architecture of the room. The choice is yours. The mistake many people make is attempting to do both. A historic, circa 1865 family room is not the place for a high-tech entertainment center. But a Colonial style built-in cupboard angled in the corner to house the television, CDs, and stereo equipment makes perfect sense for a home styled in this period and for the way we live today.

Another family with a passion for folk art chose the warmth of a large maple entertainment center that covered an entire wall. Each of these choices drew attention to itself, creating an instant focal point as well as adding to the ambiance of the décor. My own choice was to build in shelving and storage around the fireplace that allowed me to display artwork and accessories without the distraction of other details.

As you think about the decorations in your living/family room, also explore the types of activities that you do, or want to do, within those spaces. We've talked about some of them, but almost everyone has an activity that is unique

**OPPOSITE**   A recessed cabinet keeps the floor plan open while providing room for storage and style. (Photographer: Patty Minnick; room courtesy of Charter Homes and Neighborhoods, Lancaster, Penn.)

**BELOW** To make this vintage 1865 family room make sense for today, we crafted a corner cupboard that is a beautiful reproduction of the period, but outfitted to handle a television and other media discreetly. (Photographer: Lori Stahl; Interior Designer: Sharon Hanby-Robie)

to their interests and hobbies. For example, one family with four young children had expectations that seemed to exceed the design of the room. They wanted homework, piano lessons, television watching, and computer use to all be done in this space.

The first thing I noticed is that there wasn't a table large enough to accommodate homework. The room had six windows that streamed sunlight. I love sunlight, but it made watching television or using the computer incredibly difficult. By rearranging the floor plan we were able to place a dining-sized table at one end of the room that made homework easier and also created a place for family board games and pizza parties. Then we added shades to each of the windows so that light could be controlled as needed.

## KEEP DESIGN AGE APPROPRIATE

One client who is the single parent of two teens had her heart set on a more formal style of decoration. She felt that since the children would soon be leaving for college, it was finally time for her to be able to express her own style. With proper planning, even a semiformal style of decoration, like Neoclassic, can be family friendly with the right fabrics and scale of furniture.

I like to call this style of decorating Informal Elegance. It is achieved by making strategic choices. For example, if you want your teenagers to keep their feet off the cocktail table, then try using a glass-topped table and fill it abundantly with accessories. That said, if you want your teens to hang around with you, accommodate them with an ottoman or two so they can get comfortable. Comfort doesn't have to forgo style. Your style can express itself with personal touches and accessories. The family room is the place where I encourage clients to display and enjoy their treasures. This room should truly reflect who you and your family are. Accessories should tell the story of your lives.

I have always encouraged my clients to create a wall of family pictures. Recently, I had the opportunity to visit with a client several years after we first worked together on her home. She was so excited to show me how the family picture wall had, over time, turned into an entire room of photographs. She said the youngest family members would get so excited each time a new photo was added. Family pictures not only add to the ambiance, but displaying them can give you an instant mood boost. According to a National Institutes of Health Study, when moms looked at pictures of their children, the emotional parts of their brain responsible for attachment, protectiveness, and empathy lit up on MRIs. The part of the brain related to episodic memory also reacted, suggesting that the mothers were recalling those specific times with their kids.

To truly make the living room a gathering place means taking into consideration the reality of the phase or stage of life that you and your family are in. The biggest struggles and decorating disappointments happen when we expect our family members to act an age that they are not. A family with toddlers needs to soften the edges and leave lots of open space for crawling, running, and living. You can still decorate with beautiful art relics—you just have to use the walls and higher surfaces.

**OPPOSITE (TOP)**   Simple shelves surrounding the fireplace are the perfect niche for displaying artwork and accessories. (Photographer: Lynn Noble; Interior Designer: Sharon Hanby-Robie)

**OPPOSITE (BOTTOM)**   There's no compromising on style or comfort in this busy family room with plenty of room for teenagers and friends. (Photographer: Lori Stahl; Interior Designer: Sharon Hanby-Robie)

## DESIGN FOR LIFE, NOT JUST LOOKS

Fortunately, today technology allows us to have fabrics that are rich and visual as well as nearly indestructible. Fill your spaces with the things you love and you will love your spaces. Just make sure to arrange them for comfort and convenience. Your home should adapt to your life—not the other way around.

Some of my clients still like the idea of having a more formal living room as well as a family room. Many new homes being built today include a "formal room" that can be used as a home office, music room, formal living room, or even a craft room. It all depends on your lifestyle and needs. These rooms are usually smaller and tucked off the foyer.

For one client with two teenagers in the home, this space became her respite. And although this room is not off limits to her children, we designed it to completely reflect her more formal style of decorating, with exquisite fabrics. A fabulous red and camel plaid silk fabric for the draperies sets the tone for a tufted formal ottoman with Bullion fringe at the hem. A small-scale sofa in a luxurious camel and black woven tapestry provides a comfortable place to rest alongside the baby grand piano. Care was taken with each small detail to make this room the luxurious niche she desired.

Your home should not only be visually appealing but it should also enhance the quality of your life. Your home is where your children's memories are born. When they think back on their childhood, the memories should be filled with love, laughter, and time spent together— not about how they had to worry about not making a mess. Our homes should be *lived* in.

When I work with clients, I encourage them to write a mission statement for their homes.

For some, who have the gift of hospitality, their mission may be to welcome as many people as they can to their homes. For others, it may simply be to find a refuge from the hectic outside world. Each of these goals requires a unique approach to how a home is laid out and decorated. For example, a home for empty nesters who have hobbies that require a lot of space would differ from the home of a single woman who trains guide dogs. A home's mission is as unique as the individuals who reside there.

Consider writing a general mission statement for your home and then a specific mission statement for each of your most important rooms. For me, simplicity is a key element in making my home feel peaceful. To accomplish this, I chose a few larger, significant pieces of furniture with fewer treasures on display rather than an abundance of them. Less is more for me. I need my living spaces to have breathing room. I also want to leave room for future acquisitions. I believe a home should be beautiful and functional and filled with hope and encouragement for all who reside there.

## NOW DO IT YOURSELF

■ **Look for cluttered areas.** Can't see them? Take snapshots of your living spaces and analyze whether some organization is needed. I believe

that there is a direct correlation between the chaos in our home and the chaos in our lives; if either is out of balance, the other will be affected. We may not be able to control the outside world and its chaos, but we can bring a little peace and order to our lives simply by cleaning a little clutter from our homes.

- ■ **Now, refill your living room with only the items that are needed for daily life within those walls.** When possible, choose comfortable dual-purpose furniture that offers additional storage space.

- ■ **Let the artist waiting within you express herself.** Your home is the one place where you have the freedom to do so. Find something beautiful today to add to the space where you spend the most time. It will lift your spirit and make your home one step closer to truly being the home of your dreams.

# STEP 3: A Bedroom Sanctuary

Bedrooms are one of the most important spaces within our homes. French naturalist and writer Guy de Maupassant said, "The bed comprehends our whole life, for we were born in it, we live in it, and we shall die in it." A bedroom has two lives: a night and a day life. Our bedroom is the place we go for solace, love, dreams, and

**OPPOSITE** My living/family room is designed for peaceful comfort. I love the beach, so this room's style is inspired by the color and atmosphere of my favorite island shore. (Photographer: Lynn Noble; Interior Designer: Sharon Hanby-Robie)

sleep. Many of us find this the place for the most productive contemplation. It is a sacred place, too. We pray there; we create and reenergize life there; our children are conceived there. It is a powerful, peaceful, mysterious place.

As an interior designer I recognize the significance of a bedroom, which is why I prefer not to make this the first room I decorate for a new client. I feel it necessary to develop a relationship with the client first, so that I can create a space that is as perfect as their dream for it. Because so much of our lives and our dreams are attached to our bedrooms, they evoke some of the strongest emotions. I believe, especially for women, that a beautiful bedroom has the power to transform us. Men often have a hard time understanding the importance of such spaces. They struggle with spending hundreds or even thousands of dollars on bedding. Yet when they finally agree to a bedroom renovation project, they too are amazed at the difference a beautifully decorated respite has made in their lives. Not only are their wives happier with a well-designed room, but the men also benefit.

Perhaps one of the reasons that women need the sanctuary of an appealing bedroom is because it was our adolescent haven. For many girls, their bedroom was the one place where they felt safe and could be themselves without fear of ridicule. In addition, the bedroom was the only space that adolescent girls felt as though they had power or control over, and they liked controlling how tidy or messy their rooms were, what they had on display, and what music they played and how loud they played it.

I remember at thirteen choosing and hanging wallpaper for my bedroom. I can see every detail in my mind today. The lavender, pink, gold, and white floral stripe pattern showed my

**ABOVE** This room is all "girl." Pretty in pink and pretty as a picture, it's the perfect room for a princess. (Photographer: Patty Minnick; room courtesy of Charter Homes and Neighborhoods, Lancaster, Penn.)

**OPPOSITE** This cheerful Cottage bedroom is equally comfortable for men or women. (Photographer: Lori Stahl; Interior Designer: Sharon Hanby-Robie)

love for Country French style that has continued today. Even then, I preferred white furnishings, as I still do today.

The master bedroom should be a place for couples to feel comfortable. But I believe a woman needs this space to be as close to her ideal as possible. Dreams can and should come true in the bedroom. When working with couples, only a few male clients opposed soft or feminine fabrics. To most men, being satisfied with the room had little to do with style and was more related to how comfortable the bed felt.

## SEEK PEACE

You will be able to create a personal and satisfying space if you take the time to imagine a special place of sanctuary within your otherwise busy household. Visualizing your ideal sanctuary requires identifying the key qualities that will make it your personal haven. Is it cozy, elegant, or austere? Is it filled to the brim with loving memories and memorabilia? Or is simplicity your key characteristic? What type of mood do you imagine? Is it inspiring—a place for dreaming? Or is it simply a place for serenity—a place to let go of the day and relax without focus? Will you watch television, write in your journal, listen to music, or sit and talk with your children?

One of the primary goals of a sanctuary space should be to instantly transform your mind and spirit to a place of contemplative peace and joy. If it's cluttered with laundry, exercise equipment, paperwork, and other distractions, you will find yourself feeling overwhelmed and perhaps even depressed instead.

One of my clients felt her life was incredibly hectic. Her desire for her bedroom was for a total sanctuary. The colors and aesthetics were chosen specifically to create a sense of peace. For her, watching television helped take her mind off work and other responsibilities and allowed her mind to finally rest. As a result, we chose a small lingerie chest with doors at the top in which we could hide a small television with a DVD player. We also chose to incorporate a writing desk. This gave her a quiet place to write in her prayer journal about life. This

simple act helped give her perspective and peace. A sanctuary should be a place that promotes quiet so that you can hear yourself think.

Use beautiful items to evoke calming thoughts. Choose symbols that quiet your mind. As I have mentioned before, a few simple seashells can quickly help me find the sense of peace that otherwise I only find at the beach. As a child, whenever I faced a difficulty, I found solace and God at the water's edge. Sitting there was like a prayer for me. What objects help you contemplate peace? It is only with thoughtful effort that you can truly create an environment that promotes meditation and reflection.

Artwork is one object that has the power to transform. I particularly like landscapes and floral images in the master bedroom. Place artwork so that it can easily be viewed from your bed. By doing so, you can claim the mood the art suggests to you. Even in the midst of sorrow, art and its beauty can be a light to your soul.

How the furniture is arranged, the colors, the lighting, and even the sounds and scents that surround your bedroom can positively or negatively affect the mood within. Haphazardly arranged spaces give way to chaos. Your bedroom should be inviting, and with thoughtful design it can be. The bed is the focal point of the bedroom. In an ideal world, all designers will

tell you that you should be able to see the foot of the bed when you enter. If at all possible, the headboard would be placed in the center of the longest wall. That said, very few perfect rooms exist. Make the most of your room's architectural features and the views afforded by your windows, then place your headboard where you can most enjoy a beautiful view from your bed. I like to let a bedroom unfold as I enter—letting each element speak for itself and yet act as an integral part of the whole design.

## CHOOSE THE BED AND COVERINGS

As the bed is the focal point and the place where you will spend most of your time in the bedroom, it should be aesthetically pleasing and comfortable. Choosing the perfect bed is about trusting your own instincts and taste. Avoid trendiness. Design is always a step of faith into your imagination. Joseph Joubert, French moralist and essayist (1754–1824), said, "Imagination is the eye of the soul." I believe that if we allow our imagination to inspire our designs, we will give our souls the beauty they seek.

Bedrooms should be romantic but should be balanced with discipline and playfulness as

**OPPOSITE (TOP)**   I admit it, I love pink! It feels fresh and romantic—the perfect choice for our master bedroom. (Photographer: Lynn Noble; Interior Designer: Sharon Hanby-Robie)

**OPPOSITE (BOTTOM)**   The placement of the bed in this room takes advantage of the incredible outdoor views. (Photographer and Interior Designer: Lynn Noble)

**ABOVE**   I love leading the eye by the strategic placement of furniture to let spaces unfold, one into another. The placement of furniture in this bedroom exemplifies this principle. (Photographer: Patty Minnick; room courtesy of Charter Homes and Neighborhoods, Lancaster, Penn.)

our childhood when, as little girls, we dreamed of having a canopy bed. Poster beds can be strong and masculine or frilly and feminine in style. They can be draped in velvet bed curtains, or they can be light and summery in gauzy linen curtains. Undraped, they can act as an abstract sculpture or architectural element. I call this calculated simplicity.

For years I had a white, slip-covered headboard. It was originally purchased for a home I previously lived in. Last year I finally purchased a simple, yet elegant Country French bed complete with headboard and footboard. It balances the room so much better. The high vaulted ceiling of this home needed the strength and volume that this new bed provides. I considered using a pair of antique shutters in a verdigris patina as a headboard—and I would have, if I could have found them. I even considered having them custom made. But in the end I chose the carved pine headboard because it would allow me to use a variety of bedding without competing.

One of my favorite elements for a bedroom is a bench, a table, or even a pair of chairs at the foot of the bed. If you have room, a pair of chairs can give you the sitting area you desire without taking up precious space on the longest wall in the room. A table is the perfect place to keep reading material and enjoy a cup of coffee in the morning while reading the newspaper. Of course, a bench provides a place to lay your comforter or to sit and put your shoes on each morning. In my home, it's one of the places my cats like to sleep. They also find it a convenient step on their way to the bed.

The most aesthetically pleasing spaces appeal to all the senses. This is especially true for the bedroom. Your senses should be soothed and

well. An anonymous quote describes the perfect bed as being a lover: "I want a love like my bed. Someone to support me, someone comfortable, someone who will listen to everything I say and will be there to catch all my tears. Essentially, a bed is the greatest model of an idealistic love there is."

Daydream about your perfect bed. Is it graceful and draped in silk like a ball gown? Or does it have a plain and simple upholstered headboard with layers of fine woven textures? Perhaps you are dreaming of an iron four-poster bed that will bring form and architectural elements to your space. Or maybe your heartfelt desire is for a Gothic inspired hand-carved headboard with swirled columns and exaggerated arches. Quilts, tapestries, folding screens, and recessed niches can all make for inspiring headboards.

Four-poster beds are a popular choice because of the sheer variety of styles available. But I also think that poster beds relate back to stimulated. The bed is the place where you have the most flexibility to create an atmosphere of romance, tranquility, or energy simply by changing the bedding. I believe this is the place where you deserve to splurge. Fortunately, luxurious bedding doesn't necessarily mean expensive. Today's high–thread count sheets are more affordable and available than ever before. And this is one area where men and women both agree on splurging. Fine bed linens are a detail guys can relate to the minute they slip into bed.

I remember the first time I experienced a feather bed complete with down comforter and pillows. It was at a little hotel in the Swiss Alps where I stayed while traveling. I had never slept in anything so sumptuous. The memory of its comfort stayed with me for years, until I could finally outfit my own bed for the same experience.

I enjoy the flexibility of using a duvet cover rather than a bedspread or comforter. But the choice is yours. If you rarely change the cover of your bed and are content with keeping things the same for long periods of time, then invest in a quality comforter or bedspread that you love. I like to change my bedding to suit the season. Sometimes a bed in pure white is the perfect antidote to a dreary day. Other times, I need the energy of color to bring my mood up a notch or two in the bleakness of winter. For one client,

**OPPOSITE**  The simple lines of a four-poster bed make a strong impression. (Photographer: Patty Minnick; room courtesy of Charter Homes and Neighborhoods, Lancaster, Penn.)

**BELOW (LEFT)**  Layers of fabric, detailed with tassels and trims, create an atmosphere of luxury and elegance. (Photographer: Lori Stahl; Interior Designer: Sharon Hanby-Robie)

**BELOW (RIGHT)**  Textures, trims, and styles are the key to creating an interesting group of pillows that transforms a simple iron bed into a luxurious nest. (Photographer: Lori Stahl; Interior Designer: Sharon Hanby-Robie)

patterns created visual noise and made her room feel cluttered. By removing floral and other patterns from her space we were able to "quiet" the room.

Every spring I set aside one day to change my bed linens from a winter style to a fresher spring style. I love the look and feel of my crisp, spring-like pink polka-dotted sheets and a pastel colored floral-patterned duvet cover. The pure white, cotton bed skirt is hemmed purposely 3 inches above the floor, which leaves the room feeling airy and light. Seasonal changes in bedding can instantly transform the atmosphere of the room and my mood, too.

## COLOR AND HARMONY

Although I prefer soft, nonaggressive colors in the bedroom, many of my clients enjoy the power of strongly contrasting colors in their spaces. Blue is the most popular color chosen for master bedrooms. The color of your walls sets the stage for your dreams. Color is one of the strongest emotional triggers—scent is first. We will discuss color at length in Chapter 3. But I do want you to understand that in your bedroom it is important to take careful consideration in choosing a color that will enhance the mood you want to create and foster your style. Color also has a significant influence on the

attitude of your room. It can be frivolous, cozy, cheerful, romantic, serene, somber, or bright. The choice is yours. One word of caution: If the sun pours into your room, as it does in mine, it's best to keep the color on the paler side. Stronger colors look great at night, but can be agitating in full sunlight.

Remember to keep your colors harmonious by creating opportunities for contrast with different textures rather than strong colors. Each finish, surface, or material has its own way of expressing color. A shiny surface brings color to a deeper level while a matte surface can absorb the color. Rough or smooth surfaces also change how color appears. The most beautiful rooms are those where color composition includes satin, semi-gloss, gloss, and matte finishes, as well as multiple textures.

**OPPOSITE** The dramatic power of red patterned walls sets the tone for romance in this master bedroom. (Photographer: Patty Minnick; room courtesy of Charter Homes and Neighborhoods, Lancaster, Penn.)

**ABOVE** Perfect symmetry best describes this young girl's bedroom. The bed is placed strategically in the center, creating a lovely composition. (Photographer and Interior Designer: Lynn Noble)

I would never suggest that a client purchase a bedroom suite or matched collection. A bedroom needs one significant piece of furniture such as an armoire or chest to act as the second focal point. The most interesting interiors are those that appear to have evolved over time, with each piece contributing both artistically and practically, while still maintaining harmony in proportion to the space. There is something to be said for a room where unexpected tension is created by the juxtaposition of many different styles and woods that work together seamlessly despite their differences.

If you have a well-organized closet that provides most of your clothing storage, you will be able to include more interesting furnishings without worry of how much they store. Besides, the reality is that most of us wear 20 percent of our clothes 80 percent of the time. If we had the courage, we could eliminate most of the clothing we own.

I love to use built-ins, particularly bookcases. In my own bedroom, I used a mere 15 inches of depth behind the bedroom door to build a bookcase from floor to ceiling, wall to wall. That not only gave me a place for books and accessories, but also additional storage behind the doors I placed on the lower portion of the bookcase. But the best part is that it created an element of architectural interest that would otherwise not exist. It also created the perfect balance needed against the large-scale window on the opposite wall.

The most important walls within your bedroom are the one behind your bed and the one you see from your bed. These two views are critical to how your room feels. Use the photograph trick here to see if your eye is in denial of disorganization. Many clients are surprised at how a stack of books in the corner of the room can appear as clutter to the eye of the camera, while two or three neatly stacked books on a shelf or a bench can be artistically appealing.

Occasionally, a room allows me to float the bed in the center, which creates the most dramatic impression. I am working on a space like this for a client now. This octagonal room is filled with an abundance of light coming from windows, doors, and skylights. We have chosen a color that is between caramel and peach for the walls and the ceiling. The bed we have chosen is dramatic in style and presence. It will be the focal point of the room. The wall to the rear of the bed will be covered in softly toned large-scale plaid wallpaper with just a hint of iridescence to the finish. The color and sheen appeal to the feminine while the pattern itself expresses masculine—the perfect choice for this couple.

Be ever conscious of your room's light and location because it will always affect color and overall appearance. For one client who has an apartment at the beach, our color choice was specifically chosen to change as the light in the room changed. The view from the patio doors is dramatic both day and night. I did not want the color of the walls to compete with it, but to simply complement it.

## WINDOW COVERINGS

Fabrics add substantial character to a room, and beautiful fabric speaks volumes in bedrooms. From the bed coverings to the windows, fabrics make a statement that cannot be ignored simply because of the sheer volume necessary within a bedroom. For simple, smaller rooms, uncomplicated draperies work best by allowing the bed to be center stage. But for rooms with volume and high ceilings, draperies can be an important element in creating balance. My bedroom is in the front of the house. It has a very large arched window on the front wall, as well as a standard-size, non-arched window on the bed wall. It took time for me to visualize how to treat these windows because they are so different in size, shape, and proportion. I knew that I wanted to use sheer fabric, because I like the sun

to wake me in the morning. I also did not want to detract from the architectural element that the large window provides.

Simple white sheers with white floral embroidery were embellished with elegant tassel trim to become the perfect choice for my windows. A custom-made rod was necessary to maintain the arched shape of the window. A local drapery specialty shop had the rod made locally by an artist and craftsman. It was fabricated from PVC plumbing pipe, which was heated and bent to match the curve of my window. It was hand-painted to match the large artichoke-shaped finials that I chose as the finishing touch. Bell-shaped pleats gave the valance the detail needed to make this simple fabric chic yet relaxed, and were accompanied by single panels that piddle (not puddle) to the floor. (Decorators use the words "piddle" to describe a

**ABOVE** To maintain a beautiful arch above the window, PVC plumbing pipe was heated, bent, and then hand-painted to match the artichoke-styled finials. Simple sheers become elegant window dressing when embroidered and enhanced with tassel trimmings. (Photographer: Lynn Noble; Interior Designer: Sharon Hanby-Robie)

smaller amount of fabric gathered on the floor, and "puddle" to describe a larger amount.) A matching treatment gave the smaller window more of a presence, creating the perfect balance for the room. Because the windows were such a large feature in my room, choosing just the right draperies was critical to the overall scheme. Sheers have and continue to be a popular choice for bedroom draperies. Perhaps it's their soft, subtle elegance that is so appealing.

The relationship between an interior designer and a client requires trust. I remember one client who had just moved into her first home when we began to work together. I delighted in her excitement as each little detail came into place. Paint colors, furniture choices, and arrangements moved from the blueprint to reality right before her eyes. I was the first designer this client had worked with—and earning her trust took a few weeks. Her husband was on board much sooner. But she was a skeptic, which is why her positive response to each element was so rewarding. When we finally installed the embroidered sheers in her master bedroom, she jumped up and down and hugged me. She was like a little kid on her birthday. She was amazed at how two ordinary windows could be made to look so grand by simply extending them beyond the window frame. She also watched with amazement as her king-sized bed, which just a few moments before had appeared much too large for the room, suddenly came into proportion as the windows grew to create a perfect balance.

Balance is not a hard idea to grasp. Just imagine your room in the palm of your hand. Your hand is a scale. If your room is out of balance your hand will tip to the side that bears more weight. Weight can be actual or visual. Clearly in the case of this client's bedroom, the sheer fabric draperies were not a match in actual weight to the king-sized bed. However, with the window treatment, the windows visually became nearly as big as the king-sized bed, creating the necessary balance for this space.

Creating a beautiful bedroom is an opportunity to make your dreams come true. Whether you need the lift of a soft yellow-tinted room or your heart desires the romance of a rich red color, don't be afraid to make the space your own. The bedroom is the place to indulge yourself. Of all rooms, the bedroom should make you feel good.

## NOW DO IT YOURSELF

- **First decide the best viewpoint from which to position your bed.** Then consider hanging beautiful art on the wall opposite the headboard. Choose wall colors that inspire you to feel settled and happy, and fabrics that stimulate your senses.

- **Once you have positioned your bed, focus on the wall behind it.** Make it special with details such as wallpaper, artwork, or molding. Remember, it is part of the focal point composition.

- **Light control should be your first consideration when considering window design.** Fortunately, there are many beautiful options that can provide room darkening without the need for heavily lined draperies. Consider room darkening Silhouette or honeycomb shades. I have also used simple matchstick shades with a lining that provided enough darkening to please most customers.

# STEP 4: The Bath— Your Personal Best Bathing Beauty

As the demands of everyday life continue to grow, we increasingly seek a safe haven for renewal within our homes. The bathroom is one of the most logical places for such an experience. It is the place we begin and end our day, and it is the most conducive space for creating a spa-like environment. The latest and greatest in bathroom fixtures and accessories can take our imagination beyond our wildest expectations, even something as simple as candles and perhaps a whirlpool.

## TACKLE THE CLUTTER

But just as with the other rooms in your house, no matter the size, era, or condition of your bathroom, it will never be a sanctuary as long as it is disorderly. Bathrooms seem to be a magnet for clutter. We can all identify with how easy it is to accumulate a dozen bottles of

**BELOW** Restful colors and plush towels are all it takes to make this bathroom a sanctuary. (Photographer: Patty Minnick; room courtesy of Charter Homes and Neighborhoods, Lancaster, Penn.)

shampoo and conditioner, six partially used cans of hairspray or gel, and assorted salves, lotions, and potions, as well as a hairdryer with several unused attachments, three sizes of curling irons, and bottles of old prescriptions. In addition we expect the bathroom to house lots of towels, shower spray, toilet paper, facial tissue, and makeup. Cosmetics alone can take up a huge amount of space in a bathroom.

It's amazing how we can spend so much time in a room and rarely think about the clutter. Just as I have suggested for previous rooms, I want you to take a really good look at your bathroom. Use the photo trick—and start with your bathroom countertop. I know you can't help it. That long smooth horizontal space just begs for you to drop everything there. It's so convenient. The problem is that it is also a focal

**LEFT** An infusion of pink flowers not only enhances the beauty of this bathroom sanctuary, but the arrangement's abundant size also keeps us from cluttering the counter with daily potions and lotions. (Photographer: Lynn Noble; Interior Designer: Sharon Hanby-Robie)

**OPPOSITE** Fresh, white, and light-filled, this bathroom is the perfect place for relaxing. (Photographer and Interior Designer: Lynn Noble)

point in the room and disorder there makes the entire room feel cluttered.

One of my techniques for keeping clutter on the countertop to a minimum is to fill a large portion of the space with a floral arrangement. I have used this in many bathrooms. Clients love the idea of seeing beautiful color the minute they walk into a room. Flowers give us a lift. They make us feel good. My clients are also amazed at how easily they were able to find another location for all those items that used to reside on their countertops.

Another idea that I have used often for clients who have a long length of counter space is to add a pier cabinet to the middle of the counter. A pier cabinet is generally no more than a foot wide but it can be as tall as your mirror or go all the way to the ceiling. I prefer to use one that coordinates with the existing cabinets. If you can't locate one to match, a local cabinetmaker can easily fabricate one to fit your space perfectly. This cabinet with a door will provide an enormous amount of storage and keep your bathroom countertop uncluttered.

Like your kitchen, this room needs to be organized from one end to the other to get rid of everything that is no longer being used or is out of date. Banishing clutter means removing everything and evaluating its usefulness. When in doubt—toss it out. If your husband has bottles of never-worn cologne and you have perfume you don't use, toss them. Be brutal and only keep what you really use. We've all fallen prey to trying yet another new product that failed to meet our expectations.

Accept the fact that cosmetics have a shelf life of about six months. Get rid of the thirteen lipstick tubes that you have had forever. If you can't remember when you bought them or when you last wore them, get rid of them. One idea I heard that makes complete sense is to simply write the date of purchase on your cosmetics and lotion bottles when you purchase them. That way you will know when to toss them out.

Medications are another collection that seems to multiply in our bathrooms. I tossed out all the outdated cough syrup, allergy medications, and other items about a year ago. If you looked in my bathroom cupboard today, you would find it hard to believe I ever touched it. To fix this, I have decided to schedule fifteen minutes every four months to sort through the medicine cabinet.

One of the easiest ways to gain additional storage is to add it from your walls. Shelving added to the vertical unused wall space can provide all sorts of much-needed storage. Look behind your bathroom door—do you have some wall space? If the area behind your dry-wall is vacant, it's a great place to create recessed storage. A mere 4 to 6 inches of recessed space between studs can be enough to house all your bathroom toiletries. This is a rather simple project for do-it-yourselfers, or you can hire a handyman to tackle it for you.

Kitchen organizers also work great for bathrooms. The large open cavity that many bathroom vanities have under the sink can become a disaster if we don't take the time to create organized space. I attached plastic storage shelves to the inside of each of my bathroom vanity doors. I also added wire mesh basket drawers to help keep the area under the sink clean and clutter-

free. Don't forget drawer organizers. Of course, a simple cabinet designed to fit neatly around the toilet can provide amazing space as well. Even adding a hanging medicine cabinet on a vacant wall can add enough storage to reduce clutter.

## APPEAL TO YOUR SENSE OF BEAUTY

Once your bathroom is clean and clutter-free, it's time to address the ambiance. Something as simple as thick, luxurious towels can instantly transform your bath into a spa experience. My favorite place to find the best towels inexpensively is at T.J. Maxx. But thick, luxurious towels also take up an enormous amount of room in a linen closet. To help solve this dilemma in my own home, I have eliminated all but two sets of towels per bathroom. That way I only need to store one set in the closet.

Another place where I think a little indulgence goes a long way in making a bathroom feel like a spa is a beautiful rug. First, banish the matching throw rug you bought with your towels—you may keep a bath or shower mat, however. But now it's time for a real rug that will truly reflect your taste and style. Nothing anchors a room more beautifully than the right rug. A rug can be simple, chic, contemporary, or traditional. The style choices are endless. The rug in our master bathroom is a hand-tufted, cotton loop flannel, which has been sheared and brushed to give it a soft velvety touch. The ground color is a soft green with large beautiful pink and white flowers woven throughout the design. The moment I walk into the room it catches my eye and lifts my mood.

As with all rooms, color is a key element to inducing the right mood. It greatly affects our psyche. I love using wallpaper in powder rooms and bathrooms. Whether it's a simple texture or a detailed pattern, I think it adds so much personality. For our bathroom I chose wallpaper with a white background and a soft shade of green leaf pattern. It's fresh and uplifting. Although my bathroom is fairly large, the scale of the paper is purposely smaller because windows and doors chop up the remaining wall space. The smaller scale pattern on the paper helps bring the space together. A larger scale would have been visually busy. My cabinets are white; my floor is a large neutral stone tile.

Color can be blissful or energizing. I prefer blissful for a bath. Brighter colors can always be brought in through accents and accessories. This is why I almost always recommend starting with a neutral base for floors and fixtures, which are a long-term investment. Besides, you don't really want to ask

**LEFT** This cotton hooked floral bouquet rug provides a soft foundation in terms of both comfort and décor in my master bathroom. (Photographer: Lynn Noble; Interior Designer: Sharon Hanby-Robie)

**OPPOSITE (TOP)** A room with little wall space can feel chopped up and disconnected. But the soft delicate leaf-patterned wallpaper turned this space into a lovely cohesive environment. (Photographer: Lynn Noble; Interior Designer: Sharon Hanby-Robie)

**OPPOSITE (BOTTOM)** A crystal lamp reflected in the mirror of this master bath doubles the glow while creating a classical impression. (Photographer: Patty Minnick; room courtesy of Charter Homes and Neighborhoods, Lancaster, Penn.)

yourself why you chose that pink toilet four years from now, do you?

When it comes to countertops, I encourage clients to enhance the elegance by replacing a countertop with travertine, limestone, or other natural stones that can help achieve an upscale look without completely remodeling the entire bath. When selecting a stone for your countertop, consult with the experts, because many natural stones are too porous for such use and will stain easily. To locate an expert, ask your builder or remodeling contractor to recommend a stone supplier in your community. Avoid using standard retail stores because there are few real experts working in most of them. If you deal directly with suppliers, they can guide you in your selections. You'll also have the opportunity

to see firsthand full slabs of various stone, which helps you visualize how your counter may look.

Next to color, lighting is another critical component to setting just the right mood for your bathroom. You can feel a room's mood change when the lights change. Be flexible. You may need brighter light in the morning to wake and dress by, but prefer a softer glow of light for relaxing in the shower or bath. (I'll discuss lighting in depth in Chapter 5.) But at the very minimum I suggest using a generous amount of light, with a dimmer switch. Installing a dimmer lets you create the perfect ambiance for dressing, applying makeup, or just relaxing. By providing

frosted shades on lighting, you will keep it glare free, which is much easier on the eyes.

While we are talking about new installations, if your bathroom fan fixture is old and

**BELOW** The deep tones of the faucets are complemented by the rich dark colors of the curtains and planter. (Photographer: Patty Minnick; room courtesy of Charter Homes and Neighborhoods, Lancaster, Penn.)

**OPPOSITE** A tumbled stone floor is the perfect match for the marble-tiled shower walls. A simple border of dark tiles highlights the mosaic inset, which is complemented by the rich dark stain of the shower stool. (Photographer: Patty Minnick; room courtesy of Steven L. Edris, Builder, Lancaster, Penn.)

noisy, consider investing in a new one. The new ones are whisper quiet. How can anyone relax or hear the soothing music playing on the CD with the racket of a noisy fan? This is a simple but important way to bring a little quiet to your sanctuary spa.

Even if you do not want to take out a major loan and completely remodel your bathroom, there are inexpensive ways to improve it. One we have already talked about is to replace your countertop. But faucets also make a statement. Faucets are like jewelry for the bath. They can accent or transform a space, depending on your choice. In fact, some faucets even come with interchangeable accents for the handles that can easily change the mood of your room.

Whenever a client is making changes in a bathroom, I look for the opportunity to incorporate universal (or as I prefer to say, "lifestyle") ideas. We all benefit from universally accessible design. And the older we get, the more we will appreciate appliances that make our simple daily tasks easier. Of course, living on only one floor is the best choice for accessibility, but other simple ideas can help make life easier. Replacing a standard faucet with a new lever style is one of the simplest ways to accomplish this. Today the style choices for lever or C-shaped handles are endless. Designers realize that lifestyle doesn't simply mean old and disabled. New design in bathrooms and kitchens allow children, pregnant women, or people using wheelchairs to get closer to a sink or counter. All of us benefit from good design that is accessible to everyone.

Showers have nearly become a lifestyle in themselves. It's not unusual for a client to combine a rainfall showerhead for relaxation with a regular showerhead for daily quick showers. A hand-held showerhead in my opinion is a

must-have. Not only does it make the shower more accessible for family members of every age, but it also makes cleaning and rinsing the shower so much easier. Many new homes now are built with walk-in, curbless showers that easily accommodate a wheelchair. If you are considering a major remodel in your bath, this is a good idea to consider. Also consider making the interior at least 5 feet by 5 feet to fit a wheelchair (and a helper, if needed).

I also believe that every tub or shower should incorporate grab bars. All of us could use a hand up every now and then, and there are many

**ABOVE** The contrast of light and dark make this bathroom feel fresh while maintaining a sense of traditional Shore style. (Photographer: Lynn Noble; Interior Designer: Gail Dunn)

**OPPOSITE** This bathroom is designed to stimulate the senses, yet it is practical for real living. The varied counter heights easily accommodate daily tasks. (Photographer: Patty Minnick; room courtesy of Charter Homes and Neighborhoods, Lancaster, Penn.)

attractive options to choose from. But I caution: Do not purchase a grab bar with a smooth polished surface. They are incredibly slippery when wet. Choose a satin nickel or slip-resistant surface finish. Secure grab bars to studs or blocking in the wall surrounding the tub, toilet, and shower interior so they do not pull out when in use.

For major remodels, the bathroom vanity is important not only for storage, but because it sets the mood for the room with its style. If you are neat enough and brave enough, you can try one of the new open-and-airy style vanities. A simple woodwork table with a slatted shelf below can be the perfect choice. I prefer to always give my clients some hidden storage. A Shaker-influenced cabinet with doors and drawer on the upper third and an open shelf below gives the room a lighter feel without the worry of clutter. Furniture-style vanities have replaced most of the old standard-style cabinets. They allow more flexibility in style and character, just as in your other rooms.

For a restoration of an 1865 building that was being converted to a bed-and-breakfast, we chose to use antique dressers as vanities. The home originally had no bathrooms and there was barely enough space in the new bathrooms to add showers and toilets; putting the sinks in the bedrooms, where there was much more space, seemed a logical solution. We fixed the first drawer of each dresser so that it could not open and then recessed a porcelain sink into the top. The antique dressers blended perfectly with the bedroom décor. For a client who was building a home, we chose to incorporate beautifully curved feet for the cabinets in her bathroom. In addition, rather than simply using standard square corners on the cabinetry, we designed a soft and sensually sweeping curve to wrap each interior corner.

Another idea that is gaining in popularity with bathroom cabinetry is to vary the heights of the countertop areas. My husband is nearly 6 feet 4½ inches tall. I am 5 feet 2. This is an idea that absolutely makes sense for us. It also makes sense as a practical way to provide easy, comfortable access for children as well as adults. The counters can be positioned between 25½ inches and 42 inches above the floor.

The goal is to create spaces that make sense for your life and your family. Think about how long you plan on living in this home. Then let your imagination inspire the design of your bathroom. Ultimately, it should be a beautiful and efficient mix that meets your daily wash-up

needs as well as providing a sanctuary spa to soothe the troubles away.

- **When everything is completely removed from your linen closet, vanity, shower, and bath area, give your bathroom a complete cleaning.** Grab your box of cleaning supplies and start in on all the nooks and crannies: tile grout, behind fixtures, inside cupboards—even take the shower-head off and give it a good cleaning. Sort items and discard out-of-date ones before putting things back into this room. Find new spaces to keep all the items that have been stored on your countertops.

- **Refresh the room with a luxurious rug, new towels, and flowers on your newly cleaned counters.** As money allows, replace old fan units, plumbing fixtures, and lighting to give your room an inviting lift.

# STEP 5: The Beauty of a Home Office

The beauty of a home office is that it is in your home. Sadly, the beauty of most home offices stops there. Often people who decide to move their office to their home don't take the time to plan or invest in furnishings and organizational systems that make sense. Instead, they grab an old table or desk and a couple of mismatched filing cabinets and set up work. And it's not until they find themselves unable to function—or worse yet, unable to find necessary paperwork—that they consider making changes. I'm sometimes amazed at the condition of some home offices. I know they wouldn't tolerate such a situation in a professional work environment. So why tolerate it in their home?

Personally, I love working from home. I resisted it for a long time because I was concerned that I would have trouble separating home life from work life. I didn't, but some people do. However, I don't think the act of moving your office to your home creates the separation issue. Many who can't separate their work from their home life experience that problem even when their office is outside the home.

## SELECT A LOCATION FOR YOUR OFFICE

One of the important reasons that working from home is so enjoyable for me is that I planned well for it. When I built this home I seriously considered my business and other interests, knowing that they required very specific storage requirements. I also knew that I need a lot of natural daylight for spaces to be functional and productive. My husband, on the other hand, does not. He keeps his window shades closed all day. To accommodate my desire for daylight, I selected a space in my basement where the topography of the land allowed me to incorporate patio doors and windows.

**OPPOSITE** A busy mom manages her business from an easily accessible workstation on her kitchen counter. (Photographer: Patty Minnick; Interior Designer: Sharon Hanby-Robie)

**ABOVE** Even if you don't own the company, you can treat yourself like royalty in your own home office. (Photographer: Patty Minnick; room courtesy of Charter Homes and Neighborhoods, Lancaster, Penn.)

The large basement gave me the opportunity to finish off a portion as office space as well as create abundant storage in the unfinished areas. If and when I sell this home, the offices will easily convert to bedrooms and a recreation room, with kitchenette and full bath.

Having a quiet environment was also one of my top priorities. I need quiet to concentrate when I am writing. I can't even listen to music when writing. Because my office is in the basement, when my husband chose to move his office home, we located it on the second floor of our home. We do have an intercom system that allows us to easily communicate with each other, while the separation of space gives us each plenty of undisturbed quiet.

My assistant's office is placed in the open area outside my office, where we work together on projects. She has patio doors beside her desk to provide daylight and I have a nice window in my office. I planted a lilac bush just outside my window to give me something beautiful and calming to look at when I am feeling stressed.

The first important decision regarding a home office is simply choosing the right location for your office. If, like me, you need quiet to concentrate, choose a location that is away from the hub of family and noise. If you can't handle a lot of interruptions, then be sure you are not too conveniently located to the rest of the household. This will discourage family members from simply dropping by whenever they have a free moment. One article I read suggested posting your work hours on the door to remind family members that, although you are home, you are working.

If on the other hand, you are invigorated by the clamor of life going on around you, perhaps a simple office located in the alcove of the family room or kitchen can work for you. Just be honest and realistic with yourself. One client attempted to work from the dining room table. It was a disaster. He was simply unrealistic in thinking that he could actually keep two boys and a big dog quiet every time he was on the phone. We finally moved him upstairs to make life happier for everyone concerned. It's not uncommon to start your home office in one room and then move to another.

For another client, we converted the hardly used dining room into his office. We placed double doors with a window transom above, to close off the main entrance of the dining room. Then we placed a glass French style door on the smaller doorway. That gave the young children of the family the security of being able to see Dad while not disturbing him. The double doors gave him complete privacy from the front foyer—making the transition from dining room to home office architecturally seamless.

My home office also doubles as a second guest room. It has an old brass bed that works perfectly with my Country style L-shaped desk, hutch, and bookcase. To make the most of the closet in my office, I raised the clothes bar a few inches to accommodate my filing cabinet, which is placed in the center of the closet. There is still enough room on either side of the cabinet to accommodate guest clothing. A hand-painted trunk at the foot of the bed provides storage for additional blankets. A small antique wicker table and two chairs add ambiance as well as a place for guests to read or enjoy a cup of coffee in the morning. All in all, it works out perfectly both as my office and as an occasional guest room. The key to this harmonious existence is organization.

## DECIDE WHAT FURNITURE YOU NEED

When evaluating your needs, start with the basics. Will this be a full-time or part-time office? Part-time usually requires less room. Be considerate of your working style. I need a lot of room whether I am writing or working on a design project. I always spread out my research materials so that I can easily see them when working. Will you need bookcases? How many files and what type? Do you want open or closed storage on your desk? Only you know the type of things you will need to accomplish your work. So even if you are working with a professional designer, be specific and honest about your needs and your work style.

Your desk is a critical decision in form and function. As the focal point of the room, the style of your desk will speak volumes. A sleek Contemporary writing desk has a completely different personality than an antique hand-carved, French style writing table or a Sheraton style secretary desk. How your desk is positioned also affects the overall image your office presents. A wall organized with filing, storage, and desk space can be inviting—or it can become a visual nightmare. It depends on your working style. For one client, we purposely chose to design a system that allows nearly everything to be easily hidden behind doors. This allows her the freedom to leave unfinished work without having to see the mess. The small

**ABOVE** The artwork adds a modern touch of color and inspiration to this casual and trendy home office. (Photographer: Patty Minnick; room courtesy of Charter Homes and Neighborhoods, Lancaster, Penn.)

**OPPOSITE** Every nook and cranny was well planned and customized to accommodate music, books, and of course a little work as well in this home office getaway. (Photographer: Patty Minnick; Interior Designer: Sharon Hanby-Robie)

40-inch open writing area is sufficient for the task without leaving room for clutter. As you plan your home office, give serious consideration to the best position for your desk in terms of light, accessibility, and visual appeal.

There are a few items that I truly believe we should never skimp on: filing cabinets and chairs. Neither of these are cheap investments if you are purchasing high-quality versions, but they are more than worth it. Did you know that professional desk chairs come in petite, standard, and large sizes? They do. And most of them have as many as six or seven possible adjustments so that you can make them fit ergonomically, as close to perfect as possible. The older we get, the more important a chair becomes.

So skip the local office supply store and go directly to a commercial office equipment dealer to become familiar with all the options. You have to sit in a chair to know if it is right for you. As I said before, my husband is nearly 6 feet 4½ inches tall. He kept insisting that I should just pick out a chair for him because he didn't want to be bothered with the selection process. I told him that he had to be kidding— I am more than a foot shorter than he. Sure, I could have guessed—and if the chair didn't fit properly, I would have heard about it the rest of my life! I won't pick out something so important without the client's trying it, and I wasn't going to risk doing so for my husband. He finally agreed to take the time necessary, and it was well worth it. I have never heard him complain about being uncomfortable at his desk. When I first suggest that clients try commercial furniture, they resist. Most of us have this image of the "ugly" office chair in our heads. Don't let this keep you from pursuing a commercial office chair. You can easily find a commercial chair that fits your sense of style as well as your body. The commercial furniture industry is delightfully in sync with today's design style preferences. A commercial office equipment dealer can also be a great place to find a bargain. They often have a scratch and dent section, as well as used furniture. This is also a great way to find a quality filing cabinet for less. A few dents here or there don't matter, but an easily gliding drawer that is capable of holding a few hundred pounds of paper is important.

Your home office should make you feel good to be there. It should be efficient, but it should also reflect your personal style and taste in decorating. One savvy, Contemporary client with a passion for art used artwork as the focal point in her small office to create impact. The piece of art is nearly as long as her desk, which is built along one wall. With daylight streaming in from the side door and window, the art is made even more impressive by the natural illumination. And although her desk faces the wall, she has something very beautiful to inspire her as she works. Her office's Contemporary style is consistent with the style throughout the rest of her home, as it should be. There's no reason that our home offices can't be as inviting as the rest of our house. Making your home office personal is one of the perks of having an office at home.

## ORGANIZE YOUR WORKFLOW

Paperwork alone can become overwhelming in any office if you are not prepared to deal with it. This is especially true if you are also running your home from the same space. I do. I pay bills, prepare taxes, and manage my home from my office. Because I am an author and an interior designer and work for QVC television, I am in fact managing three different types of business from here as well. It's actually quite common for those who work from home to be involved in various pursuits. I guess it's the entrepreneurial spirit that most home-based

businesspeople have. We like to try and do a variety of things. It keeps life interesting, but it can also be an enormous challenge to contain, organize, and maintain all that goes along with multiple interests. That's why good planning is necessary. After all, if you are not comfortable in your office, you will be less inclined to spend productive time in it.

Another client, who loves books, asked that I design her small space to accommodate as many books as possible. Fortunately she has a high ceiling that allowed me to build a wall system that could easily accommodate an abundance of books. I specifically took advantage of the one full wall in her space—the cabinetry goes wall to wall and floor to ceiling. We built in a little refrigerator to keep refreshments. We also created an area that accommodates an electric teakettle to make teatime convenient. Her office is light and airy. The patio doors allow for lots of light and access to her personal garden. We were able to incorporate draperies from her mother's apartment in New York as well as treasured mementos and photos. This little gem of an office perfectly reflects her personality. It is a functional beauty of a space.

A space as personal as a home office is best designed when we pay attention to color and details. Sometimes the simplest detail is wire management. In fact, it's often one of the first things I address in a home office because women can't stand to see wires and cables. For some reason, it doesn't bother most guys. Computers, faxes, copiers, printers, phones,

**LEFT** Tucked into a little niche, this home office is adorned with treasures and a needlepoint cushion to make it truly reflect the personality of the person who works here. (Photographer: Patty Minnick; Interior Designer: Sharon Hanby-Robie)

and lighting all need to be planned for electrically in order to make your office not only operate easily but look professional as well. I almost always recommend that clients invest in an all-in-one fax/copier/printer just to keep the pieces and the wiring to a minimum.

One of the simplest ways to manage the tangle of wires is to use an inexpensive system such as an interlocking wire channel with a snap-off cover that can be installed at the bottom of a wall, like a baseboard, so you can easily hide wiring. It's available for existing homes or new construction. (For more information on cord management, select the home office link at www.rockler.com.) Other ideas to consider are wire master channels with a snap-shut latch that gets your smaller wires and cable under control, or a flexible tube organizer to put an end to tangled cables and wires. If your desk doesn't have a grommeted hole for channeling wires (a drilled hole with a plastic insert to make the surface look finished), install one. Organizers and grommets are available from almost any woodworking hardware supplier. Lighting, as in all rooms, is a matter of importance in your office. I apply the principle of using three different types of light: ambient, task, and accent. (See Chapter 5 for more on lighting.) I consider a good, full-spectrum desk lamp a necessity, particularly if you work evenings or early mornings. These are available in an endless variety of styles. I chose a simple foldable lamp that is also perfect for sewing, quilting, and other crafts. I like it because I can easily move it about the room, depending on whether I am reading or working at my desk. For one client I recently located a great full-spectrum lamp—which doubles as a docking station for MP3 players, PDAs, and portable satellite radios—with two

light heads and therefore twice the light to cover a broader area of the desk.

Home offices have stepped up to technology, and although high-tech items such as computers and copiers may not be beautiful to look at, they can be tempered with personal accents. Use art, color, textures, and collections of photos and other memorabilia to fill your office with all the homey touches you would use in any other personal space. Always give yourself something beautiful to look at, whether it's a view of the backyard or a simple sculpture—it will help soothe your spirit from the stress of work.

## NOW DO IT YOURSELF

■ **Choose a space in your home that best suits your working style.** Invest in office equipment that fits both your personal style and comfort level. Organize your workflow so that you can easily find what you need when you need it. Don't forget to surround yourself with art or personal collections that inspire you to feel creative and beckon you to the room when it's time to work.

# STEP 6: Laundry Rooms and Mudrooms

When I was a child, our family of eight washed clothes in a wringer washer and hung clothes on a line to dry. Thank goodness we have come

a long way since then. The laundry area has been elevated from a utilitarian room to a pleasing environment for homeowners. In the 1970s, the washer and dryer began to find their way out of the dark, dank basement. We tried placing the laundry in the kitchen, but it created a noise problem. Next we moved our machines to a closet or niche on the second floor, which in most cases was simply too small to manage the piles of laundry and cleaning supplies. It also created an obstacle course in the hallway. Now, finally, we are designing inviting rooms near the kitchen, which can accommodate not only the laundry but other creative activities as well.

Multipurpose rooms are possible because washing machines and dryers have also evolved throughout those years. The latest models offer high efficiency and the capacity to wash sixteen pairs of jeans at one time. They are ultra quiet, which makes it possible to place them almost anywhere you want them. And that has influenced a new practice of actually designing two laundries in a home—a smaller laundry near the master bedroom and a full-size laundry somewhere near the kitchen.

Some laundry rooms are doubling as craft or sewing rooms, mudrooms, or potting areas as well. If humidity can be eliminated from the laundry room, dual use of the room for other functions is quite successful. Many of the experts discourage the combination of laundry rooms and mudrooms because they are two distinctly different disciplines—one involving cleaning and one that is extremely messy. That may be true, but I do believe you can incorporate both if you plan well. In fact, I am seeing more washers and dryers being incorporated into mudrooms in the back entry hall than ever before. They are ingeniously hidden behind French doors, or even built into hutch-style cabinetry with fold-back doors. Back door entrances are usually such a waste of space. But if you enlarge the width and create a mudroom/laundry in them, they make a lot of sense for the way we live today.

## ALWAYS ORGANIZE

Of course, organization is absolutely necessary in planning a beautiful utility room. A well-designed laundry room with designated shelving and storage can be the center of activity. Start by evaluating your laundry room and your appliances. For a major remodel, plan for new size requirements that today's appliances require.

**OPPOSITE**  This laundry room is made sophisticated and beautiful by using cabinetry to match the adjoining kitchen. (Photographer: Patty Minnick; room courtesy of Charter Homes and Neighborhoods, Lancaster, Penn.)

**RIGHT**  With a little planning, an entryway becomes a practical mudroom with slate tile floor and much-needed storage. (Photographer: Patty Minnick; room courtesy of Steven L. Edris, Builder, Lancaster, Penn.)

You may also want to consider rearranging the floor plan at the same time, and that may require some restructuring to accommodate plumbing.

When it comes to storage, take into consideration whether you work best with open or closed storage. I always try to place cabinetry above washers and dryers to match the kitchen cabinets. It's a great place to conveniently and safely store laundry detergent, fabric softener, and spray starch, as well as other cleaning supplies—out of sight and out of reach of little ones. If you

have the room, incorporate a floor-to-ceiling wall cabinet as well. This is the perfect place for craft or sewing supplies. Fill it with bins and baskets that are well labeled; make it easy to keep things organized. For one client, we actually added a small writing desk to her laundry room with file racks along the side wall. She said that she could always count on quiet time at this desk because no one would bother her in the laundry room for fear of being put to work!

Many laundry rooms now incorporate a retractable clothing rack for drying clothes and a closet that can accommodate either out-of-season clothing or bulky winter coats and jackets. Of course, we can always use extra counter space for folding clothes or crafting. Cubbyholes or built-in hamper-style baskets are a great way to eliminate the piles of laundry on the floor. Simply sort your dirty laundry directly into a cubby. Built-in ironing boards are great for a larger laundry room. But for smaller ones, I prefer to hang the ironing board either on the wall or on the back of the laundry room door. I love to iron in my kitchen, so having the ironing board easily accessible is nice. Yes, I actually do love to iron and to indulge in the luxury of a bed made with freshly ironed sheets. I iron in the kitchen where there is an abundance of daylight. I put on a favorite CD and enjoy the process.

Many homes are being built with a shower in the laundry. Others not only include a shower but a powder room as well. This is not my favorite idea. I find it cumbersome and not necessarily compatible. I like the idea of having a place to wash the dog, but I am not sure this is the place for it. I have seen floor sinks incorporated into mudrooms and that seems more appealing. They usually have wood grates that cover the actual drain and a basin that can easily be removed for cleaning.

I have stopped recommending the old style (ugly) washtubs for laundry rooms. Most folks like the idea of having a large capacity sink for cleaning petite pets, repotting plants, soaking clothes, or cleaning paint brushes. Today, there are many more attractive and functional styles available. One of my favorites is the Big Single from Moen. It is a single bowl that is 33 by 22 by 10 inches. It's available in stone-like composite material or brushed chrome. The perfect companion faucet would be a pullout hose style that would accommodate almost any task. But don't be dismayed if you have an old-fashioned washtub. Just do as I have done for many clients and make it beautiful by adding a gathered skirt around it—by doing so you also gain hidden storage beneath it.

Mudrooms continue to grow in popularity. It makes me wonder why we ever stopped using them in the first place, because they simply make good sense. The best-designed mudrooms result from observing your daily entering and exiting habits. I'll bet you would be surprised at how many activities evolve around your back door. In places like Minneapolis and other cold climate regions, a mudroom is incredibly useful for storing bulky winter clothing and boots. If designed properly, it can create an airlock or buffer to keep cold air from entering the main part of the house. It also helps to keep belongings from being scattered throughout the house. The goal of any mudroom should first and foremost be durability and ease of maintenance. I love using lathe boards or paneling on mudroom walls because it can take a beating far better than drywall. The floor also should be durable and easy to clean. Laminate flooring or tile work well.

Some basics for a functional mudroom include a bench with storage underneath, and a hook, cubby, and basket for each child or member of the family to keep shoes, boots, hats, and coats in. I recommend a 36-inch-wide door for mudrooms simply to make entering easier. I also think this is one of the best places for the family activity calendar.

You don't need a lot of space to create a workable mudroom. For one Chicago client who desperately needed a mudroom but didn't have an entire room to dedicate to it, we created a mud zone along the wall in the hallway leading from the garage to the kitchen. We had cabinetry built to match her kitchen and created individ-

ual open lockers for each child with boot/shoe storage on the bottom and a shelf wide enough to sit on on the top.

Of course, daylight makes any room better and reduces eyestrain, increases our productivity, and cuts down on electricity costs. Adding a window to your laundry room can completely change your attitude about the chore of laundry. If installing a window is not possible, consider instead installing a Solatube skylight. The newest version provides a 24-inch square of natural light. I recently used one in a client's walk-in closet and she is thrilled. If all else fails, add interesting lighting to the space. A pair of pretty pendant lamps suspended above the washer and dryer can accent artwork hung on the walls while also creating a beautiful distraction. I have also used "window" murals successfully in a windowless laundry/mudroom. Window murals are wallpaper that has been printed with a picture of a window and a scene. They are cut to the size of the printed picture, so they are very easy to hang. I just recently chose a window mural with a view of a Tuscan hillside for a client in a town house. There are hundreds of window styles and views to choose from—formal, cabin, country, island, and cottage are just a few. One of my favorite sources is York Wallcovering at www.yorkwall.com.

## USE BOLD COLORS HERE

Years ago, when I was designing model homes for builders, I always decorated laundry rooms in bright cheerful colors. I painted one room coral and added a floral wallpaper border, pretty accessories, and even a wicker chair. This laundry room was also the back entryway. The builder said that every woman that walked through it complimented it. Then just a few years ago, I did a Parade of Homes model for a builder and convinced him to let me paint the mudroom/laundry in a deep pink color. We used the new improved large capacity washer-dryer combination and included a sink that automatically launders your handwashables. Once again, I used a beautiful wallpaper border and lots of pretty accessories. I was even able to create an area for potting plants.

Not only did the house sell the first day of the Parade, but I gained several new clients. They all commented on the pink laundry room. One of those new clients said she hired me specifically because she loves pink and knew that I would be able to make her new home perfectly pink for her. And we have. Her kitchen/family room is painted her favorite shade of pink, despite the objections of the architect and builder. I believe that there is no reason why a "utility" room can't be pretty. Most homeowners spend an estimated five to seven hours a week in their laundry rooms; they should at least enjoy the view while they work.

Your laundry room should be decorated according to the style of the rest of your home—particularly your kitchen, if it is located nearby. A home that flows comfortably from one room to the next in style, character, and colors is more pleasing on the eye and mind. Smaller rooms such as laundry rooms and mudrooms are great places to use color as your primary statement. Don't be afraid of bold, beautiful color for your walls. Whether you prefer paint or wallpaper, take your style up a

notch above your comfort level and experiment with a bolder version of your décor. Work from the color palette surrounding your laundry and then choose a shade that intensifies those colors for your laundry room theme. If you love lavender, consider painting a wall shelf purple to brighten the laundry. Put the accent on details to make the most of your style. Artwork and other wall accessories can say a lot with a little. Again, the key is to echo what you have used in surrounding areas of your home—with a bit more punch. An area rug can also make a significant statement in a small space. Choose one that matches your mood. If you are worried about durability or water spills, select a beautiful outdoor rug. They can literally be hosed down and are incredibly durable.

There is no reason you shouldn't really love your laundry room. Make it a beautiful, light-filled space where function has been disguised as style.

## NOW DO IT YOURSELF

- **Make your laundry functional by adding cabinetry for storing unsightly bottles of detergent and bleach.** Give your laundry room a fresh coat of paint that is just a bit brighter than one of your three main color décor choices.

- **Get your crafts organized.** Even a small closet or corner niche can become Craft Central with a little help from clear plastic bins and organizers. Don't forget to label boxes and storage baskets so that you can easily find what you need and gain more time for craft fun.

■ **Establish a dropping ground for shoes, boots, coats, and other family belongings at the most used entryway of your home.** Consider the use of durable wall surfaces that can take a hit or two and not leave a dent in this busy traffic area. Take advantage of vertical space by adding shelves, hooks, and even shallow closed cabinets or open bins so every family member has his or her own organizational space.

# CHAPTER 3

# Designed for the Senses

- **STEP 1: SCENTS AND SENSIBILITIES**
- **STEP 2: LIFE IN LIVING COLOR**
- **STEP 3: TOUCHABLE DÉCOR**

The most aesthetically pleasing rooms appeal to us through sight, smell, sound, and touch. The scents, colors, and textures of our homes are all an integral part of the atmosphere. Yet we are rarely aware of how these elements affect our senses because our response to them is so innate. We don't consciously think about how a smell affects us—it just does. Sometimes the effect is positive and other times negative, but either way, scent is a vital part of what we experience in different environments.

These sensory components trigger emotional and physical responses from our minds and bodies. We might feel chilled, despite a warm and comfortable temperature within a space, and not realize that it's the icy blue color of the walls and décor that is causing our chill. We might prickle or even get goose bumps when our skin comes in contact with an unusual texture. And despite the fact that we thought the room was beautiful, it may leave an uncomfortable impression, although we can't quite discern why.

Creating beautiful and inviting spaces requires understanding your own response to each of the different sensory elements. So let's explore some of the ways to fill your home with design elements that appeal to the senses.

# STEP 1: Scents and Sensibilities

Fragrance is a powerful tool in design because smell is the strongest of the senses when it comes to triggering negative or positive emotions. How a place smells greatly affects how

you feel about it. Think about a place where you instantly felt comfortable. It might have been your grandmother's home, a church, or even an outdoor park. Most likely you can associate a certain scent with that place—a good smell. It might be the smell of freshly laundered clothes or an apple pie baking in the oven.

Now think about a place that you didn't like—a place that made you feel uncomfortable. Can you remember what it smelled like? Certain smells easily trigger your mind to remember specific environments. What scent do you most associate with a movie theater? Popcorn, of course. How about a bakery? Most of us would say freshly baked bread. My elementary school was next to a bread factory. The minute I smell baking bread, I am transformed to the school yard. Our memory library begins accumulating scents from birth. We store our

**OPPOSITE**  Inhale deeply—I'll bet you can smell the delicious aroma of freshly baked apples and cinnamon. Scent is the strongest emotional trigger. Sometimes even a visual image alone is enough to evoke an emotional response. (Photo: MontesBurksCreative—Santa Fe)

**LEFT**  A single rose creates a heady scent for this Moroccan dining room. (Photo: MontesBurksCreative—Santa Fe)

values, feelings, and emotions in memory banks that can be triggered by a scent.

The idea of interior aromatic design is not a new idea. The ancient world was amazingly adept at creating just the right scent for the occasion. People in that time also used scent to enhance the quality of life—with healing scents, calming scents, and inspiring scents. One of the most elaborate systems for interior aromatic design was in first-century Rome where the emperor scented his palace for a party. The carved ivory ceilings in his dining rooms reportedly were fitted with concealed pipes that sprayed mists of fragrant waters on guests below. Panels slid open to shower guests with fresh rose petals. Although it's not quite so elaborate, the Bellagio Hotel in Las Vegas has its own scent that permeates the air, which includes carnation,

jasmine, and Bulgarian rose. Even the fountains are scented with this unique fragrance.

Egypt's penchant for incense and other ointments is legendary. When King Tutankhamen's tomb was opened three thousand years after he died, it still gave off a faint odor of frankincense. According to the book *A Complete Guide to the Healing Arts* by Mindy Green and Kathi Keville, the Great Pyramid papyrus manuscripts record the use of fragrant herbs, oils, perfumes, and incense, and the Babylonians made cubes of incense with ground gums, honey, and plants. Even the Bible provides recipes for holy anointing oil using myrrh, cinnamon, and calamus mixed with olive oil. Frankincense and myrrh were brought to the Christ child because these spices were considered more valuable than gold. And the ancient Greek world used rich fragrances to scent their homes. *A Complete Guide to the Healing Arts* also tells the story of how at Delphi, "the oracle priestesses sat over smoldering fumes of bay leaves to inspire an intoxicating trance."

## FRAGRANCES CAN REVIVE AND RESTORE US

Most experts consider the first century AD to be the time when aromatherapy was developed as a science. Greek pharmacologist Dioscorides wrote descriptions for more than six hundred plants and a thousand different medications in his five-volume work *De Materia Medica.* The science of aromatherapy—using plant and floral fragrances to heal and refresh the body and mind through our sense of smell—can easily be adapted to our home environments. The unique essence of each flower or plant triggers the brain to release chemicals that can reduce pain and relax and calm the body. Cleopatra used pillows filled with rose petals to induce sleep. The Romans added lavender to their baths as a balm to soothe sore muscles and relax their spirits.

We know that floral fragrances can enhance our moods and health. For example, lavender and roses are known for their calming effects. Lily, lilac, and sweet pea are known to invoke feelings of romance. But certain scents can actually increase your ability to learn. In a 1995 study at Chicago's Smell & Taste Treatment and Research Foundation, people exposed to good smells, especially floral scents, learned 17 percent faster. And people in offices filled with fragrant flowers worked more efficiently.

## FIND ODOR-CAUSING SOURCES

We are usually unaware of how our emotions are being affected by the odors we encounter. We simply don't analyze the effect of fragrance unless it is an unusually strong scent. Our senses are also more attuned to scents that indicate danger than those that delight the senses. We sniff milk before drinking it. We notice the smell of smoke almost instantly.

We are far more discerning of visual stimuli than of olfactory stimuli. We also get so used to the scent of our own home that we can no longer smell it. We may be only vaguely aware of what our home really smells like, because the more time we spend there, the less we will distinguish its unique scent.

Whenever I visit a new client, I try to pay particular attention to how the home smells the minute I walk into it. The next time you are away from your house for some length of time, take a moment to simply smell your home when you return. Or, if you dare, ask a good friend how your home smells. Unless you know there is a problem, you can't fix it.

Household cleaning products, pets, tobacco, food, mold, and mildew all contribute to the

**LEFT** Lavender calms the mind and spirit. (Photo: Montes-BurksCreative—Santa Fe)

**OPPOSITE** A ceiling fan is a beautiful and effective way to disperse fragrance throughout your home. (Photographer: Patty Minnick; room courtesy of Charter Homes and Neighborhoods, Lancaster, Penn.)

negative odors in your home. Add candles, air fresheners, and deodorizers and you can create an unpleasant combination of scents. Simply attempting to mask odors in your home with heavily perfumed products makes the problem worse. Did you also know that according to *Energy Design Update* newsletter (the leading resource for news and developments relating to energy-efficient residential design and construction), a hot car gives off carbon monoxide gases for up to twenty minutes? By closing your garage door immediately after pulling in the garage you could be allowing these gases to infiltrate your home—the same holds true for a hot lawn mower.

Heading off odors in the home requires determining the source of the problem. Moisture is usually the cause of most musty odors, which can be described as moldy, damp, smelly, cheesy, or simply rotten. All of these aromas stem from a common source—water. Usually, getting rid of the water will get rid of the odor, if the odor is mildew related. But of course, you will also have to thoroughly clean any affected areas or items.

Sweaty windows are sure signs that you have a moisture problem. Sometimes simply installing a ceiling fan and operating it in reverse (counterclockwise when looking up at it) can be enough to solve the humidity problem. The action of the paddles will force warm air down from the ceiling, drying out the windows almost instantly.

Poorly ventilated bathrooms, laundry rooms, and kitchens can also be a source of moisture problems. Ventilation fans that discharge moisture to the exterior of your home are critical to removing moisture from everyday activities such as showers, baths, cooking, and drying clothes. Even something as simple as hanging wet laundry indoors or having an open aquarium can create a problem with dampness.

Abundant moisture can cause mildew and fungus, and that will cause big problems if left untreated. Mildew is both unhealthy and destructive to your home and your furnishings. If you notice surface discoloration on your furniture, this usually indicates that you have a mold or mildew problem. Mold thrives on natural fabrics and materials. Mold and mildew often appear as a discoloration, which may be white, orange, green, brown, or black. These stains can also be found on your upholstery, under carpets, behind cupboards, on framing, in crawl spaces, and in attics. Deformed wood surfaces such as warped or cracked wood may also be an indication of either too much moisture or too little moisture. Decay or rotting wood is a sign of advanced moisture damage. The ideal indoor humidity registers between 30 and 50 percent RH (relative humidity). You can measure your home's RH with a hygrometer, available at most hardware stores and home centers.

A possible solution to moisture issues is to simply install quiet, externally vented fans in kitchens and bathrooms. Or you may consider a whole-house ventilation system. For cold surface moisture, such as sweaty windows, seal the leaks and then insulate with additional glazing that seals around the edges. Of course, increasing circulation will also help to dry out moisture. Even something as simple as keeping a lightbulb on may be enough to warm up a confined space. Also check for blocked furnace vents. A last resort is to use dehumidifiers, which I use in my basement. Dehumidifiers are a last resort because sometimes they remove too much moisture, which can cause other problems.

Once you have eliminated the source of the odor, the next step is to eliminate the smell itself. Masking the odor is only a temporary solution. Fortunately, products are available that can eliminate odor without adding to it. I'm fragrance sensitive, so this is a very important issue for me. One product that I like is called Fresh Wave. It's an all-natural spray that removes household odors without adding fragrance. It's nontoxic and nonhazardous, which makes it perfect for kitchens and bathrooms. If like me, you have cats, it's also perfect for the litter box area.

I also open at least one window each day. Even in the winter, I open a window just a crack, to allow fresh air in. With two cats, I try to be very aware of how my home smells. In addition, I have two air purifiers—one upstairs and one down. I was thrilled when recently a carpet-cleaning representative commented on how fresh my home smelled. He was surprised to find that I have two cats.

## ADD THE PERFECT FRAGRANCE

The future focus for home fragrance and household products will be custom fragrances that can be adapted to create an ambiance and enhance the mood in our home environments. The artistic and aesthetic designers will influence formulations, as will the researchers who study how fragrances affect mood and performance. Home ventilation systems will soon have the capability to dispense scents into the cleaned and purified air that they produce. In the near future, home accent designers will be able to fashion lavish, fine fragrances that will create memorable sensory experiences within our homes. These fragrances will be designed to evoke moods of tranquility, beauty, luxury, creativity, and romance.

How your home smells says a lot about you. And soon you will be able to have your own personal scent to create a welcoming home environ-

**BELOW** Colors combine with rich fabrics, lush trims, and a cachepot of flowers to make this Country French dining room inviting. (Photographer: Patty Minnick; Interior Designer: Sharon Hanby-Robie)

ment. Also available will be unique "destination" scents that capture a natural environment such as a jungle or a mountaintop. If you can't actually travel to a specific destination, you can experience the aroma of such a place by using designer scents that capture its atmosphere. Such scents are already being used in resort hotels and by the rich and famous; it is only a matter of time before they are available to the rest of us. On a much smaller scale, Glade, Dial, and other companies already produce mini-fan scent enhancers for the home.

Soon ambiance-enhancing fragrances will no longer be an indulgence, but an integral and fundamental part of decorating the home. Fragrance will become a rudimentary part of our overall personal wellness and environment. You will choose a specific fragrance for each room along with the rest of your décor. Everyday scents will become more complex, with fantasy- or romance-invoking fragrances for the bedroom and rain-forest scents for the kitchen and bathroom. The next time you think about redecorating a room, don't forget to include an interior aromatic design as well to enhance the overall design experience. Although these advanced scents are not yet available, you can purchase fragrant home sprays in many scents. It's simply a matter of finding your favorite. I use a fresh linen scent in my bedroom and a floral scent in my powder room.

## NOW DO IT YOURSELF

▪ **The first step to enhancing the scent of your home is to take an honest sniff to learn what visitors smell when they first step into your**

**house.** You may need to leave your home and visit a coffee shop for an hour or two before your "sniff test" to get a pure reaction to the scents in your home.

■ **If you detect mold or mildew, act quickly to remove the source of the problem.** You may have to seal windows, install fans, or replace leaky fixtures. This step is critical to both your health and the structure of your home. If mold is detected behind the walls, you will need to call professionals who treat this specific problem; look under "mold remediation" in the Yellow Pages.

■ **Once the source of the odor is addressed, remove any existing residue of bad odor with cleansing agents.** On solid surfaces, such as bathroom walls and tub areas, a mixture of bleach and water cleans mold and mildew with little effort.

■ **Now you can focus on adding the sensory smells that you want to enjoy.** Visit Ultra International Limited at www.ultrainternational.com to learn several ways to add appealing fragrances to your home, such as air fresheners, candles, household products, pet care products, personal care products, potpourri, soaps, and detergents.

# STEP 2: Life in Living Color

Claude Monet (1840–1926) once said, "Colour is my day-long obsession, joy, and torment." I think that most of us can empathize with this statement. We love color, but many of us are afraid of it and as a result avoid it. As I wrote in *Inspired House* magazine, color stirs emotions. I've seen people react both physically and emotionally to the colors that surround them, whether they were aware of it or not. Color is a physical expression of our emotions; it tells the story of our past and opens opportunities for our future. Every moment of our lives is surrounded by colors—colors that either positively or negatively affect our experiences.

The effects of bold, dramatic color are far-reaching and they cannot be ignored. Color can motivate, de-stress, improve one's disposition, and even help control appetite. So why are so many people afraid of choosing or using it in their decorating plans?

The trouble is that some people aren't even sure what colors they like. Others are afraid to commit to a specific color even when they know they love it. I spoke with a woman recently who would love to use color in her home but is terrified of making a mistake. Many people say they are overwhelmed by all the choices. A recent article said that the human eye sees more than two million colors! I agree that number is overwhelming. Sadly, even though few would say that white or beige is our favorite color, a study by May Department Stores found that 45 percent of bedrooms have white or beige bed linens, and 60 percent of kitchens have white or beige everyday dishes.

In interior design, just as in art, harmony results from a pleasing arrangement of colors. But our response to color is influenced by a combination of education, exposure, culture, and our individual ability to see color. Our personal histories, our life experiences, and even our religious affiliation affect how we respond to

**ABOVE**  The creative application of bold color expands and illuminates this small media room. (Photographer: Patty Minnick; room courtesy of Charter Homes and Neighborhoods, Lancaster, Penn.)

color. For example, in some religions, red is used for sacred items, while for others purple is used.

All of these influences play a part in how color affects us individually. We each have our own physical and psychological reaction to color. For example, if as a child you were severely reprimanded in a green room, you may have an adverse reaction to green rooms although con-

sciously you no longer even remember the original event. I believe that we experience color on an emotional level, which is why color has the power to affect us so dramatically.

Our reaction to color can also be influenced by age, gender, and socioeconomic status. A University of Texas study found that women experienced more depression in white, gray, and beige offices, while men reported feeling depressed in orange or purple rooms; people living in nursing homes often have lost much of their ability to truly appreciate the nuances of color.

Cultural influences also affect our choice of color. In China, older citizens avoid yellow because it evokes memories of Mao Tse-tung, who led China's Communist revolution and took office in 1945. Yet young students in China love yellow. Vacations to various places will impress you with color schemes unique to those cultures, such as the rich terra cottas of Santa Fe, New Mexico; the bright and colorful palate of Mexico; or the soothing whites and blues of Greece.

In the music world, people often talk about tone color. Different instruments are said to evoke certain colors. According to jazz composer Maria Schneider, "A trumpet evokes red, trombone evokes yellow, and saxophone blue." Just as musical color affects how you feel, the

**BELOW**  A neutral palette sings with the use of colorful accessories that lend sophistication and whimsy to this family's recreation room. (Photographer: Lori Stahl; Interior Designer: Sharon Hanby-Robie)

**OPPOSITE**  The amethyst color sets the tranquil mood for this master bedroom sanctuary. (Photographer: Patty Minnick; Interior Designer: Sharon Hanby-Robie)

visual impact of color makes you feel a certain way. Research has shown that red makes our hearts beat faster. Blue is calming. Yellow enhances concentration, and green refreshes. Because of the associations we have with colors that appear in nature, some are considered cool (green grass, blue water). Others are warm (red fire, yellow sun).

Warm colors such as red or orange actually make your body temperature warmer; cool colors such as blue or gray can make you feel cooler in temperature. Yellow, orange, and red are also said to inspire conversation by sparking emotions, with red being the strongest and most forceful. Orange applies less pressure and yellow merely suggests. And all colors contain other colors. For example, red may have a blue or an orange base. Pink may have a yellow or blue base. Recently, when I was doing a room makeover for television, I gave the painters the corresponding numbers for the amethyst paint for the walls. I arrived the next day and found walls that were bubble gum pink instead of amethyst! After the shock wore off, we realized that the paint store had forgotten to add the blue base to the paint—which made a huge difference.

In addition to mental associations with color, physical responses to color exist. Light energy stimulates the pituitary and pineal glands that regulate hormones and our bodies. The response to color is so powerful that the color pink has been used in jail cells to help control behavior of inmates. Alexander Schauss, PhD, director of the American Institute for Biosocial Research in Tacoma, Washington, has said that pink is a tranquilizing color that saps energy—even for those who are color-blind!

Color is powerful. Studies by a Cornell University psychologist found that the NFL's Oakland Raiders and the NHL's Philadelphia Flyers—whose uniforms feature black—are penalized more frequently and judged to play more aggressively than teams that do not wear black.

## FIND YOUR COLOR PREFERENCE

Knowing which color you are drawn to and understanding your own response to color can give you the ability to use color to positively influence your life—both physically and emotionally. I recommend working from the color palette of something you love. It can be a scarf, a painting, carpet, wallpaper, or anything that uses the colors that make you feel good. From this, choose your three main colors.

As you develop your color scheme, consider

Before

the value of the colors (their relative satura-tion), which can make a difference. Never mix a dark-valued color with a light-valued color. For example, a pale peach just doesn't seem right with a strong green. The weights of the colors are too different. Instead use pale colors with pale and strong with strong.

You must also understand how color affects the proportions and size of a space. Warm col-ors *advance*, making a small room appear even smaller. In a larger room, they make the space cozier. Cool colors—blue, green, and purple—*recede* and make a room appear larger. Using color correctly can also direct the focus of a room. For example, newer homes with their soaring ceilings can be problematic; it's difficult to make them feel cozy. But by using bold color

on two opposite walls, you draw the eye toward the adjacent wall, making the room feel cozier.

Even people who seem most afraid of color overcome their fear once they grasp which colors make them smile. We found that one of my clients was drawn repeatedly to purple. I don't mean pretty pale lavender. I mean purple in all its bold glory. She even asked if we could paint the entire first floor of her new town house purple.

**OPPOSITE**   Before: Without any contrast, the details of the molding in this room are lost in a haze of white. (Photographer: Patty Minnick; Interior Designer: Sharon Hanby-Robie)

**BELOW**   After: The bold russet red color draws your eye to the detailed molding and fireplace mantel to create a dramatic effect in this cozy family room. (Photographer: Patty Minnick; Interior Designer: Sharon Hanby-Robie)

After

Before making this decision, I analyzed the living space. The open floor plan of her home meant that only one room, the dining room, actually had four walls. One wall had a beautiful big window, and two walls had large openings to other rooms. The fourth wall had a large china cabinet placed on it. These features minimized the amount of exposed wall space, which meant that the purple color would not necessarily overpower the room. Each time I met with my client, I showed her a color palette that had a strong purple as its base. She continued to respond positively and never once winced. Eventually I became confident that she could actually handle living with the bold shade of purple, so we decided to go for it! We even painted the trayed ceiling in the dining room purple. We used fresh bright white for the trim, which perfectly complemented our base color. As the painters began applying this color, my client was certain they would respond with shock. Instead, they loved it. The stunning purple is the perfect background for this client's Southern formal style of decorating. It feels traditional yet exciting. Everyone is amazed at her bold choice, and they even seem to envy her courage!

## USE A COLOR WHEEL

Before we get started on selecting colors, here's a brief explanation of the color terminology designers use. *Hue* is what we mean when we ask "what color is that?" For example, when we talk about colors that are red, yellow, green, or blue, we are talking about their hue. *Chroma,*

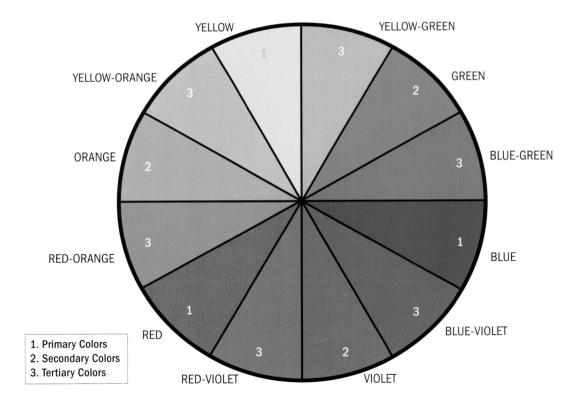

1. Primary Colors
2. Secondary Colors
3. Tertiary Colors

or chromaticity, is a matter of how "pure" a color is. It refers to the absence or presence of white, black, or gray in the color. *Tone* is a matter of how a color "differs" from the original by adding other colors. If white is added to a color, the lighter version is called a *tint*. If a color is made darker by adding black, the result is a *shade*. If gray is added, each gradation gives you a different *tone*.

Mixing colors is not really as difficult as it seems. I often tell clients that I can make any colors work simply by using something to pull them together. A painting, a rug, a sculpture—almost anything can be used to make colors work together beautifully. That said, a few simple rules will keep you from making big mistakes in combining colors. In selecting colors for your home, begin with the colors you like, and then think of how they can play into your color scheme. A color scheme is generally composed of three hues, one of them a contrasting accent color that adds visual excitement to a room. The easy way to be sure that colors will be harmonious is to use the color wheel.

Colors are defined as primary, secondary, or tertiary. Primary colors—red, yellow, and blue—make every other color in the spectrum. Secondary colors are those that are equal combinations of two primary colors: purple (red and blue), green (blue and yellow), and orange (yellow and red). Tertiary colors are made by mixing a primary and its adjacent secondary color in equal proportions (red-orange, yellow-orange, yellow-green, blue-green, blue-purple, and red-purple).

**OPPOSITE**  According to color theory, a good color scheme uses two colors opposite each other on the color wheel. These are called complementary colors. (Illustrator: Patty Minnick)

According to color theory, a good combination is one that uses two colors opposite each other on the color wheel. These are called *complementary* colors. For example, purple and yellow are considered complementary colors, as are red and green. Start by simply selecting your favorite color as your main color, and then choose the color directly opposite it as your accent color. When using complementary colors, remember that each hue will look more intense than it would if shown with a related color. It's also a good idea, when using bold colors for large expanses, to choose a shade or two lighter than shown on the paint color card, because darker colors will appear even darker when seen in large amounts. Also realize that paint usually dries to a darker shade and that the sheen of the paint will also affect the color. The shinier the finish, the lighter the color will appear.

Contrasting colors are a great way to show off artwork. A dark wall will make a painting appear lighter. By choosing a color from the painting for the wall, you can create an accent wall that highlights the painting. Then choose a different color for the rest of the walls.

Colors that sit side by side on the color wheel are *analogous* colors. Green, yellow, and orange are all analogous colors. You can be assured a harmonious color scheme simply by choosing neighboring colors. Start by choosing your favorite color and then look to either side of it for your next two colors.

Monochromatic rooms can be works of art with a single color. The key is to add depth with tints and shades, which are the lighter and darker version of the same color. Use a variety of patterns and textures to create interest when working with a monochromatic color scheme. I like monochromatic color for spaces that are disjointed and lack cohesiveness. A single color is unifying and creates visual cohesiveness. As I mentioned before, my bathroom is divided by windows and doors, but the small-scale, soft green vine-patterned wallpaper creates an illusion of interconnectedness.

Over the years, one of my biggest challenges has been figuring out which colors are best for each client. When it comes to choosing colors, most people are able to tell me what they don't like, but are not necessarily able to articulate what they do like. Sometimes they really do know—but are afraid of committing to something that they will have to live with for such a long time.

Often people will simply choose to be "trendy" because it's easier than guessing at what is right. But the problem with simply following trends or someone else's color choices is that you end up with a room that you may be completely uncomfortable in. If you put me in a blue room,

for instance, I will become cranky. So no matter how trendy blue is, it simply won't work for me.

Through years of working with clients and watching them respond to color, pattern, and texture in their most intimate of atmospheres—their homes—I have developed a fabric swatch test that is particularly helpful in this process of defining color preferences. I show them samples of fabric from various color schemes, patterns, and textures. What began as a simple fabric swatch test has now become a tool I use with new clients. I call this test my ink blot test because it gives me so much information—far beyond what I expected when I first started using the swatches. Through this test, I can determine what colors clients find most appealing, and also discover their level of formality, style preferences, and pattern and texture preferences. For the test to succeed, they shouldn't think about or analyze the swatches, but simply respond from their hearts. The swatches they respond to positively are put into a pile and the rest are discarded. When we are finished processing the swatches, people are amazed at how accurate and consistent they have been in their heartfelt responses.

You can try this test at home or at a wallpaper store. Simply start by flipping though sample books. It's important to look at patterns and styles that you normally avoid. By expanding your horizons, you give yourself an opportunity to broaden your sense of style. Often we simply fall back on what is familiar rather than taking the time to find out if something else out there might be better.

As you go through the samples, make your decisions quickly. Don't second-guess yourself. Don't worry about where you might use it or how much it costs. That is not the point to this

test. The point is to simply respond to the visual impact of each sample. Once you have finished reviewing the samples, analyze those you responded to in a positive manner. Are the colors you chose predominantly blue or green? Are they bright or soft in tone? This will tell you a lot about your personal style. It is important to keep the hue or shade (strength or paleness) of colors in balance when decorating.

## FIND YOUR OWN COMFORT LEVEL

Next consider the level of formality of the samples you have chosen. Are they formal, such as silks and brocade patterns? Or are they informal with rough-textured weaves? Are they damask? What type of patterns, if any, did you choose? Are they floral, geometric, or simply textured? How many patterns did you choose? Your choices will give you insight into how simple or how busy to make your décor.

Are the samples representative of Traditional or Contemporary style? Is a specific style reflected in your choices, such as Shaker or English Manor? If you have chosen several pat-

**OPPOSITE**  Color flows from one wall to the next, uniting this living and dining room; the result is a cozy yet expansive space that invites dining and conversation. (Photographer: Lori Stahl; Interior Designer: Sharon Hanby-Robie)

**ABOVE**  Two of the strongest color preferences are green or blue. One of these fabric boards is preferred by people who favor the color green, and the other by people who favor blue. Which one most appeals to you? Hint: If you prefer the board on the left, you are a "blue person"; if you prefer the board on the right, you are a "green person."(Photographer: Patty Minnick; Interior Designer: Sharon Hanby-Robie)

terns that could be considered either Contemporary or Traditional, this may indicate that a combination—Transitional style—of decoration should be used. My own personal style is a mixture of Country French and Contemporary elements.

The results of this test will last your lifetime. Trends may come and go, and our taste may become more refined, but basically we are who we are and we are not going to wake up tomorrow a completely different person with different responses to color and pattern. My

**LEFT** The casual yet elegant sophistication of this Country French dining room invites you to relax in style. (Photographer: Patty Minnick: room courtesy of Charter Homes and Neighborhoods, Lancaster, Penn.)

trends do offer exciting new combinations that you may not discover on your own. Just keep in mind that colors and trends are continually evolving, and every season new ones emerge.

Recently designers have focused on using colors that induce a sense of hope, such as strong bluish pink, happy yellows, geranium reds, and warm orange. They have found that people consistently respond to colors that give them a sense of optimism.

The latest color forecasts are calling for more complex colors; "multihued" is the term being used. There will be pearl-grayed colors (with a hint of gray tint in them) and "dirty" or "tinted" pastels. Colors will appear to be elusive—not easily defined. We are currently moving away from bold colors toward a more neutral or sophisticated palette. Loud colors are becoming softer, more subtle. Butter Cream and Frosted Orange are just over the horizon, as is Eucalyptus, a cloudy grayed green, and Glaze, a mocha color. Skin-toned and cosmetic shades are part of the new neutral camp for wall colors and fabrics. Yellowed peach tones, beiges, pinks, lavenders, and browns are among the range of hues that reflect the trend toward skin-toned colors.

Purple is predicted to explode over the next few years. Blue will continue to gain a strong presence, especially aqua blue, which is watery and particularly good for home fashion. There are actually twelve blues being forecast, ranging from aqua blue to robin's egg blue to Tiffany blue to sky-reddened blues. The fol-

goal with this test is simply to give you the confidence to trust your own instincts.

I also encourage you to put all family members through the process. Children innately respond to color. Allowing them to choose the colors for their own rooms will give them a sense of ownership and pride. And that, in turn, will help make their rooms a pleasurable place to be.

## TRENDS IN COLOR

Too often, clients want to use the most current trend in colors. I discourage this because I know that within a few months a new set of colors will be predicted for various reasons. But if you enjoy making changes to your home frequently, color lowing color schemes will be popular: robin's egg blue/teal, or robin's egg blue/mallard, or robin's egg blue/periwinkle, or Tiffany blue/mallard, and so on. Deep colors will be clear and rich—think espresso and chocolate brown. At one time, black was considered the main bold neutral. Then, just as in clothing fashion, brown replaced black. Now navy is replacing brown.

Oranges will replace red and will range from juicy orange to burnished copper. Pinks will be softer, merging with oranges found in nature from coral reefs and sun-filled skies. Yellow will shift to lower chromas. Warm neutrals—ivory, cream, dark browns—will be clustered together to emulate luxury. Greens will be driven by nature with clearer and cleaner looks. Think spring leaves. Of course, by the time you read this there will have been several new color forecast predictions.

So how should you respond to all these new trends? The key is in knowing your personal "best colors," and buying bedding, linens, pillows, and accessories when those colors are in style. Otherwise, you may have to wait another seven to ten years before they are back in vogue. In the end, I believe that color is one of the most powerful tools we have for enhancing the quality of our lives. Use it abundantly and joyfully to make your life a little more beautiful!

## NOW DO IT YOURSELF

■ **Be alert to your moods and positive feelings when in certain rooms, and notice the color of those rooms.** Awareness is the key to developing a color palette that will enhance the quality of your life. What three colors make you feel the happiest? Use them as the foundation of your scheme, and then freshen your décor with secondary color choices for seasonal change.

■ **Visit paint and wallpaper stores or home stores where you can pore through wallpaper samples, paint colors, and fabric swatches to select your favorite colors.** Remember, this assignment is not about price or even choosing a pattern or color for a specific room. This is about finding colors that make you smile! Let your heart be your guide.

■ **If you see trendy fabrics and colors that you love, buy them when you see them.** A new color combination will be released soon. What matters is that you surround yourself with the colors you personally love.

# STEP 3: Touchable Décor

It's difficult to resist touching something beautiful. We love to hold soft cuddly kittens and stroke the smooth worn surface of sea glass. When we shop for produce, we touch it and squeeze it. When we shop for clothing, we caress the fabric. If it feels too stiff or rough, we cringe and move on to another choice. We choose lipstick not only for its color, but also by the way it feels on our lips. We like just the right amount of moisture and gloss—but we don't like "sticky" lips.

Our homes offer an opportunity to introduce appealing tactile sensory elements. How does your home feel? Think about it with your eyes closed. Could you identify specific items in your home simply by touching them? Most of us can easily identify many of the textures within our home. Yet they may not all be pleasing to feel. Imagine feeling your way around a room within your home.

In your living or family room you will encounter a variety of sensations. The hard, smooth surface of a formal table and a well-worn hewn surface of an antique chest offer very different sensations. As you sit on your sofa, consider the comfort level. The cushions

**BELOW** Soft down-filled pillows add a decorative touch as well as comfort to my living/family room. (Photographer: Lynn Noble; Interior Designer: Sharon Hanby-Robie)

**OPPOSITE (LEFT)** Silk, cotton brocade, sequins, and fringe—what a beautiful combination of textures. (Photographer: Lynn Noble; Interior Designer: Sharon Hanby-Robie)

**OPPOSITE (RIGHT)** Flowers and seashells make me smile and give my room a sense of wonder and peace with their intricate textures and details. (Photographer: Lynn Noble; Interior Designer: Sharon Hanby-Robie)

should have enough softness for you to sit comfortably while still supporting your weight. Accent pillows can be beautiful with prickly sequins and rough buttons, or they can feel incredibly soft and touchable if filled with goose down. Many of us love to squeeze a pillow as a form of comfort. It simply feels good.

Our entire body is sensitive to how things feel because the sense of touch originates in the bottom layer of our skin, the dermis. The dermis is filled with lots of tiny nerve endings that translate information about the things with which our body comes in contact. The nerve endings carry this information to the spinal cord, which then sends messages to the brain where the feelings get registered. Some areas of the body are more sensitive to touch than others. Our tongue carries pain receptors well, but is not as good at sensing hot or cold. That's why it's so easy to burn your mouth. The least sensitive part of your body is the middle of your

back. The most sensitive areas are your hands, lips, face, neck, tongue, fingertips, and feet.

I believe the most beautiful, comfortable, and welcoming environments are those that appeal to all our senses. No matter how good a house smells or looks, if the surfaces that you sit on or lie on are hard and unyielding, it won't feel cozy or comfortable. And surfaces that are sticky or unclean will also affect how we feel about the space. Clearly touch is incredibly important in our overall perception.

Rooms that are texturally rich can invite conversation or calm the spirit simply by the way they feel. Textures that are interesting invite us to explore them with touch. As we feel them we are delighted. Layers of texture such as stone, marble, wood, shells, or even plants invite us to touch them, and by doing so we are rewarded with a deeper, richer experience of a room's décor. It is only when our homes appeal to our senses that they truly become an environment that is comforting to body and soul.

Just as young children comfort themselves by holding on to their blankets and rubbing them against their cheeks, we have a natural instinct to touch and feel objects we encounter.

There are ways to improve the touchability of every room within your home. Regardless of your decorating style, you can always find elements that can instantly make your home more inviting to touch. The kitchen is a good place to incorporate different textures to make it more appealing. Kitchens were designed for touching. Just think about all the kitchen surfaces that your fingers come in contact with. Countertops can be made of anything from concrete to diamond-brushed granite, to laminate or wood, or even stainless steel. Each of these is not only functional, but presents a different type of tactile sensation. I read about one

**ABOVE** The beauty of wood, granite, steel, and porcelain create an interesting array of textures for this classic Shore kitchen. (Photographer: Lynn Noble; Interior Designer: Gail Dunn)

**OPPOSITE** This reproduction of a William and Mary style bench has been transformed for today's lifestyle into a cocktail ottoman —which is as perfect for putting your feet up as it is for serving cocktails. (Photographer: Lynn Noble; Interior Designer: Sharon Hanby-Robie)

kitchen designer who used clear resin into which he imbedded real leaves. Although you can't actually touch the leaves, you could still imagine the sensation, and that thought alone can bring about a pleasing feeling.

Kitchen cabinets offer many opportunities for touchability. Whether they are simple Contemporary or detailed Traditional, the finish surface has its own texture, from smooth to rough. Faux worm holes, carvings, intricate moldings, and of course hardware all bring unique texture to your cabinets. The door and drawer pulls offer not only an opportunity to

add a personal expression, but also an incredible opportunity to give your fingers something nice to hold on to. Just imagine holding a twisted steel/pewter door pull. Now consider what a smaller, polished-brass knob with a crystal insert might feel like, or even a large decorative, rose-shaped, crystal knob. Each of these present themselves well and offer a different sensation when they are touched.

## COVER YOUR SURFACES

Of course, your kitchen floor also has many options for different textures. Whether you choose tile, laminate, resilient wood (wood that has been infused or finished with polymers for enhanced durability), or bamboo, your floor choice should be determined not only for its look and performance characteristics, but also by how it feels underfoot. Change the feeling simply by adding new area rugs seasonally, as I do, to enhance the quality of that experience. In the winter I use a beautiful, textured, hand-woven area rug in the center of my work area. In the summer, I change it out for a hand-painted floor cloth. One adds softness and warmth. The other adds a sense of summer fun and whimsy along with a cool sensation that I find more appealing on warm days. Don't forget your kitchen table, which is yet another way to add texture and tactile detail. I have a pine farm table that has an uneven, rustic feel to its surface. My dinnerware is large in scale with smooth details that feel good to touch. They complement the roughness of the table beautifully. But when I want my kitchen to feel more formal, I add table linens. I have lots of place mats that easily work with my fine white linen tablecloth. I love playing with different textures here. Another of my favorite tablecloths is a heavier, French style woven tablecloth with fringed ends. Each adds charm and comfort that definitely affect the overall mood of the room. But they also add to the sensory experience because we touch these items each time we sit at the table. Flatware, napkins, even the glasses or cups that you choose—all can creatively channel good feelings to your brain.

If you want your family to spend more time together, try adding warm touches to your family room or living room to create a space they will not want to leave. Adding a few big decorative pillows that allow a person to sink into your sofa, chairs, or even the floor can have a big impact on how your room feels to those you hope will linger there. Consider touchable chenille, velvet, or even silk. Today silk is far more affordable than it ever has been. And nearly

everyone enjoys touching silk. I have found many beautiful, yet inexpensive, decorative silk pillows at places like Marshalls and T.J. Maxx. Currently my family room has six pillows.

Slipcovers are another easy and wonderful way to change textures seasonally. Cool, crisp linen or cotton is wonderful for warm months. And rich layers of cotton, velvet, or chenille are perfect for cooler months.

When you are considering fabrics for upholstery such as sofas or chairs, take your family pets into consideration. For example, certain fabrics are more appealing to cats. If a fabric has a rough, uneven texture, cats will not be able to resist clawing at it. I have always had pets. As a result, for the last twenty years I used only leather furnishings because leather is nearly indestructible, very comfortable, and natural. It

is never hot, sticky, or clammy and is easy to clean. And for me the most important reason for choosing leather is that cats do not claw at it.

This year I was finally ready to redo my family room and really wanted something other than leather. The challenge was to find a fabric that my two cats, which still have their claws, would not be attracted to. It took quite a bit of research and effort, but I was successful. I finally chose polyester microfiber with a smooth, nearly napless, finish. Not only do the cats not claw it, but because they don't like the way it feels they don't even sit on the sofa. (They preferred the cool sensation of the old leather sofa, even though they didn't claw it.)

I almost always recommend using a cocktail ottoman or a couple of regular ottomans in family rooms because they add softness and practicality to a room. They just feel good. Deeply tufted, soft and cushy, formal or fun, they add a relaxed feeling to your room that a hard-edged cocktail table simply cannot. Again, the fabric choice greatly influences the overall effect. I chose an imitation ostrich leather for my large cocktail ottoman. It is durable enough to serve snacks on and soft enough to put your feet up on. The frame of my ottoman is a William and Mary style aged wood with a wonderful patina. It feels old and wonderful to the touch. Even visually you can tell how it is going to feel.

Throws add texture and touchability to any room. And today there is an abundance of fabrics and styles to choose from: nubby wools; soft, cuddly woven microfiber; bulky knits; luxurious Pashmina wool; smooth, silky fabrics with long fine fringe; even beautiful tapestry or damask throws. The fabric finish, texture, and color all add to the sensory experience. And throws are one of the easiest elements to change seasonally.

Area rugs not only help define and highlight areas within your home, but they also add texture and pattern to a room. One of my favorite styles of rug is made of cotton. When woven in a combination cut-and-loop weave these cotton rugs are both durable and touchable. They are particularly appealing when the pattern is looped and the field is a cut pile. This highlights and sets the pattern apart, giving it dimension and texture. The cut portion is actually lower than the looped section, creating a wonderful textural pattern. Of course, wool and nylon offer a unique feeling as well. Today nylon is softer than ever and is often difficult to distinguish from wool. But the texture or weave of the rug is what we respond to most. The density, pile, and texture can be used to create weave patterns such as chevron, blocks, stripes, and various designs.

The construction technique also adds to the

overall feel. For example, a Saxony weave is used to create a plush or velvet style carpet. It uses short strands of yarn that are cut evenly and twisted together for a soft, smooth, formal-looking and formal-feeling rug. A frieze style weave creates a more casual, rougher-feeling rug because it uses short, durable, extra-twisted yarn that often has flecks of color. A rug woven of multi-loops is not as plush as a cut pile, but is more durable. Its touch is softer than a level loop carpet, but harder than a cut pile.

## LAYER YOUR BED WITH COMFORT

Your bedroom is the place to indulge your sense of touch. A bed dressed in layers of luxu-

rious linens offers comfort and solace. Who can resist freshly laundered sheets? I can't. And I love when they are crisply ironed. Soft down comforters, textured quilts, smooth sheets, cozy flannel, and soft blankets make the ultimate comfort zone. This is the one place where I believe it is incredibly important to explore options until you determine your own preference. Because

**OPPOSITE**    The textures are so incredibly inviting in this Moroccan style home that you can practically feel them just by looking at the picture. (Photo: MontesBurksCreative—Santa Fe)

**BELOW**   Indulge your senses with layers of luxurious linens for a truly blissful sleep. (Photographer: Lynn Noble; Interior Designer: Sharon Hanby-Robie)

sheets are what our skin most comes in contact with, they are one of the most important sensory items. When it comes to sheets, you can choose from a wide range of materials, from a polyester blend to 100 percent Egyptian cotton. Some people love real linen on their beds. Others love silk. And still others like a cotton-silk combination or flannel.

Cotton is the most popular fiber for sheets. But there are different grades of cotton, which are determined by the length of their staple or fiber—the longer the staple, the more luxurious and durable the grade of cotton. There are two levels above the basic grade of cotton: *Egyptian* cotton is the highest quality, providing the softest, most luxurious fabric and feel and *Supima* is a long, consistent staple cotton produced in the United States, which is very soft and durable.

One hundred percent cotton bed sheets will be the softest and most breathable because they are an all-natural fiber. The benefit of a cotton-polyester blend is that it will not wrinkle as much and is more moderately priced. However, polyester sheets will not breathe or absorb moisture as well as all-cotton ones.

Beyond fiber, you have a choice in the weave styles and thread counts. Thread count is the

**BELOW** Ever a classic, Battenberg lace is perfectly at home in this Traditional dining room, where it adds texture to the table settings. (Photographer: Lynn Noble; Interior Designer: Sharon Hanby-Robie)

number of threads per square inch of fabric. Assuming you are looking for the softest and most durable bed sheet set, the higher thread count will always be the best. Look for a thread count of at least 280 or higher. Today, even a 500 thread count is affordable.

There are basically three types of weaves available. A *standard* weave alternates one stitch over with one stitch under. *Sateen* (not to be confused with satin) has a stitch of four over and one under, placing the most threads on the surface and making it extremely soft, though slightly less durable than other weaves. *Pinpoint* is a stitch of two threads over and one under. This is softer and more durable than a regular weave, but not as soft as sateen.

Decorating with a soft touch allows you to express your personality while creating a delight for the senses. Whether you prefer the look of lavish Battenberg lace or the time-mellowed touch of an old quilt, steep your home in touchable textures throughout and it will always feel welcoming.

## NOW DO IT YOURSELF

- **Walk around your home and use your sense of touch to discover the different sensations within each room.** When you encounter something that doesn't feel good, think about how you might improve on it to create a more pleasing tactile experience. This is especially important for surfaces that we often come into contact with in our daily routines. Simply changing the hardware on your kitchen cabinets can make a world of difference. One client told me that her kitchen knobs felt "evil." That's how strong her negative reaction was to the decades-old hardware. Changing them immediately changed her disposition toward her kitchen.

- **Experiment with different textures to determine which you find most pleasing.** The best way to accomplish this is to walk through department or home stores using your sense of touch to guide you in discovering new textures. Then find ways to incorporate these pleasing textures into your life.

# CHAPTER 4

# Floor Plans and Compositions

- **STEP 1: THE MISSION OF COMPOSITION**
- **STEP 2: PERSPECTIVES AND FOCAL POINTS**
- **STEP 3: DESIGNING A PLAN FOR LIVING**
- **STEP 4: TOO SMALL? TOO TALL? TOO MANY WINDOWS?**
- **STEP 5: TAKING THE BASEMENT TO A NEW LEVEL**

**U**ltimately, interior design is the art of composition. *Merriam-Webster's Dictionary* defines composition as "the act or process of composing: specifically, arrangement into specific proportion or relation and especially into artistic form." The manner in which something is composed will determine whether it is pleasing or not.

There are many components to the composition of a home. Understanding each of these and their relationship to each other is critical to applying the fine art of composition in the most artistic and family-friendly way. The vision you have for your home is the driving force for this composition. Just as an artist's overall vision drives the choice of method and medium for an artistic work, your vision drives the process necessary for interior design. If you have no idea or vision for your home, then we cannot possibly begin the journey.

Your vision, combined with the functional aspects of your home, helps create a mission. This mission gives direction to creating a beautiful composition within the environment of your home. Perspective plays a vital role in determining the mission of a composition. In a debate, different perspectives can enlighten the listener and provide insights into the issues. I often learn something new from a good debate, and that knowledge gives me a better perspective that helps me come to a more informed opinion. The same is true for our homes. Another person's perspective—your husband, a friend, a real estate agent, or an interior designer—can give us a whole new viewpoint, which helps us make better or more interesting choices for our home than we might otherwise have made.

Putting together a realistic and workable plan is a critical step in creating a beautiful composition. A carefully planned design will help you determine where to start and how to proceed in order to accomplish your mission. Of course, every room has its issues. But whether a room has too many windows or not enough wall space, there are ways that you can work around the issues and still create a beautiful and inviting room.

# STEP 1: The Mission of Composition

Before you create a floor plan for a room, first have a good understanding of the mission for the room. In fact, I encourage you to create a mission statement for your entire home and then refine that mission statement for each

room as you complete your design plan. Experiencing the life you want to live is critical to learning to love your home. Often it is not the house itself that leaves you feeling short of your goals, but the choices you have made within it that cause you disappointment.

Sometimes as I begin this discussion with clients it becomes clear that different members of the family have conflicting goals, which can create strife. This is particularly true when couples disagree. For example, if you love to entertain but your spouse would rather hibernate, each of you may have a different perspective on the mission of the family room. You desire abundant seating that is arranged to encourage conversation while your husband may want the television to be the focal point of the room.

As you write a mission statement for your home, think about what's important to you. If relationships are at the center of your heart, building a home that is conducive to family and friends is one way to define the purpose of your home. If working from home defines a major purpose, as it was for an artist friend of mine,

**OPPOSITE** This room takes advantage of an attic space to create the perfect environment for crafting and working. Good planning makes it easy to keep things organized. (Photographer: Lynn Noble)

**ABOVE (LEFT)** By zoning a large studio into specific activities, the couple who created this room could enjoy working and pleasure in one space. This part of the room is designed for crafts, such as spinning and weaving textiles. (Photographer: Patty Minnick)

**ABOVE (RIGHT)** In the same room where the wife creates textiles, the husband, a home designer, has a drafting table where he designs beautiful spaces within the homes of his clients. (Photographer: Patty Minnick)

you may choose to use traditional places of your house for more creative spaces. Consider your hobbies. Cooking, baking, crafting, weaving, pottery making, gardening, and other interests all can be part of your home's mission statement.

One of my clients tends her three very young grandchildren, and they are a very big part of the mission of her home. Every decision we make is filtered through how it affects the children and their life within the home. Another client built a fabulous room over the garage for her weaving and handbag making. It is filled with light and is large enough to accommodate her husband's desk and drafting board as well. Also take into consideration new endeavors or hobbies that you might like to try in the future. One of my clients with a musically inclined child asked that I help them create space for a piano and a harp, as well as room for dance practice.

Start your plan simply by thinking practically. That means getting every family member involved. Have all family members prepare a list of things that are most important to them. As you evaluate each list, recognize that each member has a unique perspective relative to his or her age group. And although you will never be able to meet all their needs, you can take steps to meet at least one primary need for each person. As you examine your rooms, formulate an overall goal, then narrow it down, purpose by purpose, for each room. What functions must be performed in each room?

My goal is to help you blend beautiful design with functional interpersonal activities. That requires an intelligent understanding of what is beautiful and useful and what is not. As you begin to examine each room, take time to observe where the natural light is and how you can best make use of it. Explore the good and bad architectural features. What characteristics do you love? Which do you detest? What drew you to this home in the first place? It's a good idea to recall the impressions you first had of your home. After all, it is what started this relationship. (Yes, we do have a relationship with our homes.) And like all relationships, sometimes we grow together and other times we lose sight of what drew us together in the first place.

Now take the time to simply imagine your home better than it is now: not a different home, but just this home made better. Let your mind playfully run wild as you consider new ideas and new ways of living there. Don't worry about money or rules—just experience the possibilities of the space.

Formulating a plan for your room requires understanding the basics of composition. Good design is an orderly arrangement of lines, forms, masses, colors, and textures that form a beautiful composition when unified. There are no hard and fast rules that you must follow when composing your overall plan; I will share with you the habits, customs, and principles that most interior designers apply to produce satisfaction and beauty within spaces.

## WORK WITH THE LINES IN THE ROOM

Every object has a specific line, form, or mass. We use a variety of shapes to create contrasts within a room. For example, straight lines, particularly horizontal ones, are considered restful, while movement is created when we use curved lines. Rooms are composed of small and large, short and tall, light and heavy, narrow and wide, and flat and curved masses and surfaces. Textures can be coarse or smooth, shiny or matte, plain or patterned. And colors can vary in hue, tone, and chroma. All of these elements must be carefully considered and used in proportion to create good design.

When we are looking at a room, the fixed components of the walls and the floor must be evaluated and considered for composition. The wall composition incorporates a combination of architectural elements and the furnishings that you place on them and in front of them. The floor's composition is primarily a function of

your furniture and area rug arrangements. However, it is impossible to separate the floors from the wall when designing a well-composed floor plan. There is indeed a close relationship between them that directly affects the floor plan.

For example, a window or door opening can greatly affect a floor plan—sometimes negatively and sometimes positively. Understanding that perfect solutions are not always possible will keep your frustrations to a minimum. I have had a few clients who thought I should be able to wave a magic wand and make windows and doorframes appear differently. The reality is that certain fixed architectural features often prevent us from creating perfect rooms.

**ABOVE** This bird's-eye view shows how a floor plan creates perfect balance between furnishings and architectural features such as the fireplace. (Photographer: Patty Minnick; Interior Designer: Sharon Hanby-Robie)

Today's open floor plans make analyzing walls a bit complicated. So for the sake of discussion, let's start with a normal rectangular room with four walls. Each wall should be studied individually while still considering its relationship to the other three. Look for features that might create problems in design. Identify the fixed elements such as doors, windows, fireplace, built-ins, molding, and height. Also consider the texture of the wall because this too can affect other choices. For example, you might choose a smooth surface rather than a coarse one to complement a heavily textured wall.

Ultimately, when I am designing a floor plan for a room, I also do an elevation (a vertical drawing) of each critical wall. An elevation will include the fixed architectural features along with other elements that I will place in the room, such as furniture, artwork, mirrors, wall-mounted lighting, bookcases, and so on. These elements all become part of the overall composition. The key is to create *balance* and unity by arranging moveable items in harmony with the fixed architectural elements.

Other elements on walls that can create interest—as well as challenge a floor plan—most often occur in more contemporary spaces. In Contemporary design, walls are frequently broken up by large areas of windows, large openings to adjoining rooms, alcoves, and niches. This makes room planning more challenging. It

**ABOVE**   By installing moldings at the ceiling and chair rail height (right illustration), you can add a touch of elegance. Moldings can also be used to help bring a too-tall wall into proportion. (Illustrator: Patty Minnick)

**BELOW**   This sketch illustrates how to use items of differing physical weight to create visual balance. The mirror hung on the wall behind the chair balances the weight of the armoire on the opposite side. (Illustrator: Patty Minnick)

**OPPOSITE**   The illustration on the left shows what *not* to do. The small ottoman is overwhelmed by the size and weight of the wall-hung cabinet. The sketch on the right is an excellent example of proper balance.  (Illustrator: Patty Minnick)

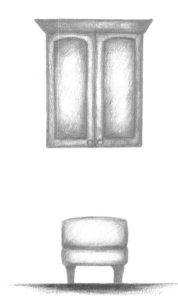

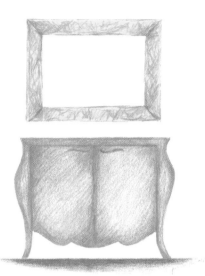

also makes it more difficult to apply the traditional design principle that states that the most agreeable wall effects are produced by three horizontal divisions of *unequal* height. All wall designs for period or historic spaces are based on this classic fundamental principle, which aims for symmetry, but this traditional rule is difficult to apply in a Contemporary space, which is broken up asymmetrically. That said, dividing a wall into horizontal elements will make it appear lower than it actually is. Therefore, never use this principle when dealing with a short wall. Obviously, if you have a very tall wall that adjoins a shorter one, then horizontal division makes perfect sense and will help bring the wall into relative proportion. For example, to bring a tall wall into normal proportion, I often add molding or shelving 9 or 10 feet above the floor.

All walls need vertical balance. There are two dimensions to balance: *physical* and *optical*. Be sure your arrangement takes into consideration the high and low furniture combined with the high and low architectural elements (windows, doors, fireplace, and so on) and creates a balance. For example, if your wall has a fireplace in the center with one window to the right side, your design has two physical elements. To create balance and symmetry you will need to add something to the left side to optically fill the space. It might be a tall chest or a painting—the goal is simply to add something of similar proportion to the window to create the balance. Think of your room or wall as sitting on a scale. It should sit perfectly straight.

## FIND BALANCE

There are two types of balance for rooms or walls: *symmetrical* and *asymmetrical*. Symmetry creates a more formal-looking arrangement.

Symmetry means a mirror image—one side is the mirror image of the other. Many people automatically gravitate to this type of balance. If this is true for you, then don't attempt to satisfy yourself with an asymmetrical design. It will never make you happy. In symmetrical design there is a strong focus on the center item (or axis) because all the other elements are reflected from there. Symmetrical balance simply means that the left and right are equal in weight— whether optically or physically. But top to bottom balance is also important. Most elements will feel more stable if they are slightly heavier on the bottom. Hence a chest with a piece of artwork above will feel more stable than a small ottoman with a hanging cabinet above.

Sometimes as a designer I purposely create something close to symmetrical—but not exactly symmetrical—for variety and interest. This is called *near symmetry*. The example with the fireplace wall and the window was near symmetry. The artwork or chest placed to the left of the fireplace was not exactly the same as the window on the right. *Near symmetry* is more versatile than pure symmetry, but still balanced optically.

*Asymmetry* is more casual and flexible, and therefore more appropriate for Contemporary spaces. Asymmetry means without symmetry. There is no mirror image in the composition. Asymmetry is harder to explain because it is more intuitive—you must be able to sense whether something is balanced. The composition either looks right or it doesn't. One simple way to tell if an asymmetrical composition is balanced is to notice where your attention goes

**OPPOSITE** This artful asymmetrical arrangement of an eclectic collection of items represents this family's passion for the seashore. (Photographer: Lynn Noble; Interior Designer: Gail Dunn)

**RIGHT** The soaring heights of this room were tamed with carefully chosen and well-placed items to create an environment that reflected both husband's and wife's styles and passions. (Photographer: Patty Minnick; Interior Designer, Sharon Hanby-Robie)

when you look at it. If you are drawn to the center of the composition, then it probably is not balanced. Your eyes should feel compelled to wander around the composition evenly.

The key to accomplishing balanced asymmetry is to have equally interesting things randomly placed throughout the design. So rather than organization being the catalyst for asymmetrical balance, the careful placing of equally weighted objects compensates for the lack of organization. Several smaller items on one side of a room can balance a single larger item on the other side, or smaller items that are placed farther away from the center than larger items can also balance a room. Sometimes a darker item within an arrangement can bring balance to several lighter items.

Quantity also affects balance. A room with too little or too much furniture can look out of balance. Rooms that are crowded can be confusing. Too many patterns can create visual chaos. Your eye will have no idea where to look first. A well-designed room will direct your eye. Every object should feel as though it belongs and has purpose. Every object should have a clear relationship with those elements near it. If something seems out of place, it probably is. Ultimately, the furnishings should feel as though they are distributed somewhat evenly

about the room. The floor and wall areas should be not just in balance but also interesting in terms of textures and shapes. Opposite walls should have an equal degree of interest.

Scale and proportion are two more very important components to good composition. This is particularly true for today's newer homes with their soaring ceilings. Most normally scaled furniture can look dwarfed in these spaces. Furnishings should always relate to the architecture in scale. But this can be problematic if you are tiny like me. The large-scale furniture simply isn't comfortable for my petite frame. To solve this dilemma in my own home, I filled the soaring spaces visually with artwork and folding floor screens. By purposely using a large piece of artwork above the sectional sofa, it created a horizontal line (the top of the artwork) that brought the room into proportion with the sofa.

## REMEMBER THE CONTEXT OF THE ROOM

The human eye is trained by experience to become accustomed to certain dimensions for certain objects that are part of our daily lives. For example, your eye has been trained to expect a dinner plate to be a certain dimension (9 to 10 inches). If you dine out at a restaurant and are served dinner on an oversized plate (12 inches), you notice immediately because it is not the norm. The same is true with home furnishings. Whenever we encounter something out of the ordinary, we notice it and often find it uncomfortable looking, even when it is perfectly proportioned for comfort. That is why context is so important. When I work with clients who have recently moved into a new larger home, I almost always have a conversation about proportions before we begin shopping for furniture, so they are prepared to accept larger-scale furniture.

Every room has a proper scale. A room does not necessarily have to have everything in the same scale to the size of the room, but it should be in proper relationship to the other items near it. For example, a large-scale candlestick can look incredibly perfect on a tall mantel, but the same candlestick placed on a low table with other low items will not look in proportion. Small-scale objects generally look insignificant when placed in a large room.

However, I often break the rules when it comes to small rooms. By choosing a few larger pieces for a small room you can actually make the room seem larger. An oversized painting or photograph can open up a room and create a vista—especially if the room has no windows.

If instead you chose several smaller pieces, they would visually break up the room into smaller portions, creating the overall effect of a smaller space. Never place a small picture alone on a big wall. Instead, group small pictures together to create mass and significance. And don't use small area rugs in small spaces; it breaks up the space too much. Instead, create a unified look with one floor type, whether it is wall-to-wall carpeting or hard flooring.

## NOW DO IT YOURSELF

- **It's time to write a mission statement for your house.** Consider your entertaining style and your family's pleasures and physical needs. Perhaps you would like to entertain more but your home is not conducive to easily entertaining large groups. This could be a mission that you work toward.

- **Design each room to fulfill its mission.** If you want your children to do homework in the family room, then provide surfaces, lighting, and the necessary tools to accomplish this goal.

- **Keep lines of furniture and permanent elements balanced against each wall.** As I suggested earlier, taking a photograph of each wall within your room can help you gain a fresh perspective about the balance on each wall. You can also evaluate whether your accessories are in scale with the spaces in which they reside.

- **Balance the weight of the room either by placing furniture in a symmetrical arrangement or by balancing items within an asymmetrical**

**pattern.** If you are more formal in style, then use symmetry to create the perfect balance in your room. If not, carefully create an asymmetrical plan for your space.

# STEP 2: Perspectives and Focal Points

Every room needs direction. And that direction should be focused around a *focal point.* This is a central object that draws the eye toward it. You should be able to walk into any room and immediately be drawn to something beautiful or architecturally powerful. That something gives your eye direction. A focal point organizes a room and helps make sense out of what could otherwise be chaos.

Some of the most frustrating rooms to design around a focal point are those that were planned by an architect or builder who looked at the house primarily from an "outside" perspective, rather than focusing on how the interior spaces would function. The results of such a perspective can be windows that are placed within an inch or two of the corner. Not only does this make it difficult to design a window treatment, but it also makes it nearly impossible to hang a drapery rod.

When windows are placed in the room to simply create a balanced exterior it can leave a

**BELOW**   All seats point to the fireplace, which is clearly the focal point of this comfortable family room. (Photographer and Interior Designer: Lynn Noble)

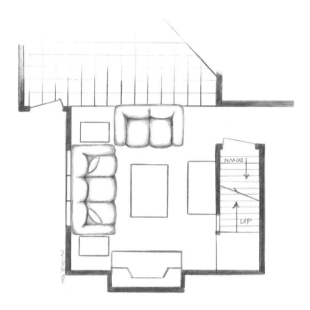

**LEFT** On paper this layout looks functional enough. However, if the architect had considered how people actually live and move within a space, it would be clear that even with standard-size furnishings, this plan is too tight to move around in comfortably. Adding 1 to 2 feet on the length and width of the walls would make all the difference between cramped and comfortable. (Illustrator: Patty Minnick)

**OPPOSITE** This restored 1865 mansion started its life as a stage stop and is now a bed-and-breakfast. The pencil post bed is the perfect focal point in a room with four windows and two doorways as distractions. (Photographer: Lori Stahl; Interior Designer: Sharon Hanby-Robie)

room with a window in a place that doesn't make sense for the interior space. That makes creating a functional floor plan a real challenge. Other problems that can occur from an "outside" perspective are rooms that don't easily accommodate furniture. When doors, windows, and other architectural features such as fireplaces break up the largest spaces of a room, it leaves no room for comfortable placement of furniture.

So much of interior design is about perspective, defined as the way in which the relationship between objects or their parts is mentally viewed. Perspective is the capacity to view things in their true relation or relative importance, and therein lies the problem. Every room can be seen from many different perspectives, and that completely affects how to approach its design. And it seems that interior designers and architects inherently see things from conflicting perspectives.

Differing views can be a good thing as long as the perspectives of both interior designers

and architects are incorporated into the plan. Sadly, very few homes are designed this way. In most cases, interior designers are not brought to the project until most of the house design has been done, leaving designers at the mercy of a single perspective. The good news is that many architects are beginning to recognize the value of an interior designer's perspective in the planning process.

Other people's perspectives also affect our home plans. For example, often when moving into a home we are influenced by the previous owner's placement of furnishings and use of space. We sometimes simply plop down furniture and accessories in the most convenient place and there they stay for the next several years. Sometimes, by luck it turns out that the arrangement and placement is the best one for the room—but most of the time haphazard placement isn't the best design.

Living in a poorly designed room gets compounded by the fact that we are creatures of habit. Once we get used to something a certain way, we have great difficulty seeing it any other way. As an interior designer, I face these issues every day. Even when I know there is a much better alternative in terms of planning, I often feel like I am fighting the law to get the client to see things from a new and fresh perspective.

Recently a client called me to help her redo her living room. I had, in fact, done this room for her about fifteen years ago. Before we went shopping for new furniture, I reexamined the floor plan and found that my original plan was still the best arrangement for her room. That meant that the new look would come from new furniture, paint color, artwork, and lighting. Soon the client fell in love with a new sofa and chairs in a warm and wonderful new color palette.

The trouble began as I attempted to get her to make the additional changes, such as paint colors, additional lighting, and new artwork in preparation for the new furniture. She was stuck in the old perspective of her room and that was making it difficult for her to move forward with the suggested changes. She decided

instead to wait until the new furniture was delivered. I said okay, but I was worried. I knew that simply placing the new bolder color furniture into a space that was previously designed for a monochromatic white color scheme was going to look wrong. And it did. Again, I attempted to get her to make the necessary changes to complete the plan. Again, she resisted. After a few weeks she decided she did not like the new furniture. No surprise. As I explained to her, if you are going to follow a plan you must complete it or you will end up with things that simply don't work together. She was trying to place new furniture into an old perspective. It never works.

Perspective is in the eye—and sometimes the heart—of the beholder. As a designer, I try to see rooms from multiple perspectives. I take the time to view a room from all angles, and I try to see spaces from the eyes of all those living within them. Occasionally, I encounter a situation where the clients are set on an idea that simply cannot be implemented within the existing space. They may dream of a cozy fireplace with big, soft chairs gathered around. But the reality is that to add a fireplace they would lose so much room space that they couldn't include the big, comfy chairs.

When working with clients, I encourage them to try to envision all the different perspectives that a room has to offer. Simply moving existing furniture around can offer a whole new view and vision for a room. Think about your living or family room. How could you rearrange it to create a whole new view?

## FIND YOUR FOCAL POINT

Some rooms have a built-in architectural focal point. It might be a fireplace, a window, or a beautifully framed view of another room.

Other times, a focal point is created with a key piece of furniture. In a bedroom, often the bed is the focal point. In a family or living room it might be the television, a piano, or even a painting. Whatever the focal point of the room, the furniture should be arranged around it.

Some rooms have focal points that are badly placed, which can make arranging furniture for practical living nearly impossible. For example, sometimes a fireplace is in an awkward corner. To place furniture around such a focal point would force you to shove the furniture toward the corner, which would leave the rest of the room empty and nonfunctional. In a case like this, I would choose to simply let the corner fireplace become a backdrop or secondary focal point and create a new, better-positioned focal point on another wall. Secondary focal points should create balance to the primary focal point. That means my new focal point should draw greater attention to itself, while the original focal point still makes sense to the activities within the room.

It's basic human nature to seek the center of interest. A specific focus allows the mind's eye to find a resting place while bringing order out of disorder. If you take the time to gaze around your room, you should easily recognize the natural feature that is the focal point. Is it the fireplace or the view out the window? Or was your eye sadly drawn to a crookedly hanging picture? Our eyes will seek out that which attracts them. Sometimes we are drawn to the distractions of a room—a misplaced chair or the clutter on a table. The goal is to create a focal point that is pleasing to the eye.

All functional rooms are built around activ-

**OPPOSITE** There's no doubt that this impressive fireplace is the focal point of this room. So we've arranged the furniture so that everyone gets a picture-perfect view from all angles. (Photographer: Lynn Noble; Interior Designer: Gail Dunn)

**BELOW** This is the perfect example of providing the ability to accomplish a task and enjoy the glow of the fireplace embers at the same time. The built-in cabinetry provides a shelf next to the fireplace where a television could easily be placed. (Photographer: Patty Minnick; room courtesy of Charter Homes and Neighborhoods, Lancaster, Penn.)

ity. Primary furniture groupings are centered on the focal point. If your primary activity is watching television, I would design your space so the television became the focal point, and arrange the furniture around it. Sometimes a room is large enough to incorporate secondary areas for other activities. For one client with a large family room, we used an entertainment center as the focal point, but added a game table at one end of the room and a piano at the other. This allowed three different types of activities while still maintaining order with a centrally located focal point.

One problem that I often encounter is an activity competing with the focal point. Today's large-scale televisions often compete with the fireplace for focal attention. If television is an important element to your family activities, then perhaps investing in a flat-screen model that can be placed into a recess above the fireplace is

the solution. Most of the time, I attempt to put the television within the same perspective (the same wall) as the fireplace to help organize and keep the room focused in the direction of the fireplace focal point. Remember that the optimal distance for viewing television is directly related to the size of the screen. (Television screen sizes are measured on the diagonal.) If your television has a 40-inch screen, then the ideal distance for viewing would be 10 feet. For smaller televisions, it might be 6 to 8 feet.

## DIRECT THE FLOW OF TRAFFIC

Traffic patterns are the other function that must seriously be considered when forming the vision for your rooms. If people can easily move through spaces, they are encouraged to use them more. When interior designers are involved in the building phase of a remodeling project, they work to ensure that a room will accomplish all their clients' goals while creating open corridors and discouraging traffic congestion.

Seating areas arranged in roughly circular shapes are the least disruptive to traffic patterns and activities. That's why corners are often used for placing large groups of seating. They naturally encourage circular seating formations. In an ideal world, when using two or more seating arrangements, they would be placed 5 to 8 feet apart to make it easy for conversation.

How much room do you need for easy traffic movement? Some say that a walkway needs

**BELOW** Tall furnishings in tight spaces (left illustration) crowd the sight line, making the space feel uncomfortable. In tight spaces, use low profile furnishings (right illustration) to keep eye level open and airy. (Illustrator: Patty Minnick)

to be 3½ feet wide. That's great if you have the space, but most homes don't. I subscribe to a minimum of 28 inches, and I design plans with as little as 20 inches when necessary. This works because most furnishings are below eye level. Therefore, visually the walkway seems larger, because nothing is obstructing your view. These tighter measurements won't work if you are placing two tall pieces of furniture on either side of the walkway, which will obstruct your view and make the space feel too small. If your situation requires tighter traffic areas, don't place a sharply cornered table where you can easily bang your shin.

Whenever I change the perspective of a room, it naturally changes the traffic flow. This is another area where some people might resist change. The reality is that some people simply have difficulty with change, even when it is beneficial. My hubby is like that; it takes him a lot of time to adjust. As you think about your room in new arrangements, consider how it will affect traffic patterns. Look for the best plan for all situations. The first concern should be function, then beauty. Work toward the rest of your goals from there. It's so important to have your hierarchy of goals and desires established before beginning to change a room.

Amazingly, sometimes your resistance to change can be easily satisfied by making a few more changes. For example, if your new traffic patterns force people to walk through an area of the home that is carpeted, and the original plan forced traffic around that area, you may be resistant to the change because you are concerned that the carpet will get ruined. But if the new arrangement solves several other problems and meets the overall objectives of the family, then it makes sense to change. When the carpet gets worn, replace it with a new rug or hard-surface flooring. The key is not to let one less important issue keep you from making changes that will enhance the quality of your life overall. In the next step we will continue this discussion as it relates to creating a floor plan for your room.

## NOW DO IT YOURSELF

■ **Find your best focal point for the room.** Remember, it may not even be actually in your room; it might be the view outside your window.

■ **Arrange seating to achieve the goal of the activity in the room.** If you like to watch television while enjoying the glow of your fireplace embers, then arrange your room to allow both activities simultaneously.

■ **Leave enough space for traffic to flow freely through the area—and the space might not require as large an area as you thought.** However, if you have a big, hulky dog or must consider the needs of someone who uses a wheelchair, make the pathways at least 42 inches wide.

# STEP 3: Designing a Plan for Living

Once you have a focal point, you can create a floor plan for your room. An established focal point is the perspective toward which your furniture will be oriented. However, sometimes activities or furniture dictate a specific perspective. For example, if you truly desire a sectional

for your family room, there probably is only one really good spot to place it. That would clearly determine which view you will see when seated on it.

Although a lot of software and Web programs will automatically create a floor plan, I prefer the old-fashioned method of hand drawing. These programs are terrific, but most of them are time-consuming to work in and are not sophisticated enough to create an exact rendering of your space. Besides, floor plans are not difficult to draw. Nor do you have to be an artist. The idea is simply to get a grasp of the space and create an orderly but interesting arrangement within it.

Start by measuring your room. First measure the four walls and draw them out on graph paper. I use ¼-inch graph paper. Each ¼ inch represents one foot of space. So if your wall is 10 feet long, then you will use ten squares to represent it. If your room has an open floor plan rather than four walls, measure the openings and designate those areas by using dotted lines instead of a solid one. Begin at one corner of your room and measure the distance to the end of that wall.

After you have drawn each wall, take an overall measurement in each direction so that you can check it against your drawing. Your rooms should be square, with corners at a perfect 90-degree angle. Here in Lancaster County, Pennsylvania, many older homes are not. When I first started practicing here, I drove myself nearly crazy attempting to make rooms square.

I finally realized that it wasn't my inept measuring, but the fact that back then, setting walls at right angles was not that important.

Once you have the basic measurements of your room drawn, it's time to add details. Locate and measure your windows on the plan. Measure them frame-to-frame: from the outside of the molding frame to the outside of the opposite molding frame (rather than the glass). Locate and measure any doorways, always using the outside frame-to-frame measurement. Then add additional elements to the layout such as fireplace, built-ins, niches, columns, and so on. Most fireplace hearths reach 12 to 18 inches into the floor area. Draw this on your plan as well.

Once your basic room is drawn, make several copies so you can play with the plan and not worry about having to erase your marks. You can either choose to work with ¼-inch furniture templates, which are available at most office supply stores, or you can draw or cut out basic shapes to represent your furniture. Don't

**OPPOSITE** Symmetry and simplicity best describe the seating area in this bedroom. The bed (you can see a corner of it in the lower left of the photograph) and the chairs all face the fireplace for balance and optimal viewing. (Photographer and Interior Designer: Lynn Noble)

**BELOW** To create your own floor plan, first draw out the space, including windows, doorways, and other architectural elements. Then begin drawing in your largest pieces of furniture first and continue until the room feels balanced. (Illustrator: Patty Minnick)

worry needlessly if your templates are an inch or two off from your actual furnishing measurements. In ¼-inch scale, a couple of inches is very hard to detect. However, if you have really tight spaces within your plan, you will need to take actual measurements and check them in your room for accuracy of fit.

## PLACE YOUR LARGEST ITEMS FIRST

Now it's time to start placing furniture within the drawing. I always start with the largest piece of furniture because generally speaking, usually only one or maybe two places make sense for it. The major pieces also are the primary elements involved in the activity in the room, such as the sofa in a family room, the bed in a bedroom, or a desk in an office. This piece should face the focal point.

Remember to focus the view toward your focal point when seated. If you do not have an established focal point, determine where the seating is best placed in your room. That place-

**BELOW**  The beauty of this Shaker style dining room lies in the view through the windows to the outdoors, which is the focal point in this space. (Photographer: Patty Minnick; room courtesy of Steven L. Edris, Builder, Lancaster, Penn.)

**OPPOSITE**  The views from one room to the next are as important as the individual spaces themselves. Create continuity with color and similar-style accessories in your public spaces. (Photographer: Patty Minnick; room courtesy of Charter Homes and Neighborhoods, Lancaster, Penn.)

ment will determine your focal point. In my living/family room, I have a wall that includes the fireplace and built-ins for media electronics. I also have a large window that gives me a view of the trees outside. I have established a bird sanctuary in my backyard, and the view out the window is important to me. I consider it my secondary focal point. I therefore placed my sofa on the wall opposite the fireplace and added a chaise at the window and another chair across from the window, where you can still see the view.

If your room provides no focal point, then simply choose the view that you would most like to see when seated. It might be a view of an adjoining space. Or you might choose to create a focal point around a beautiful painting or even a piano or other interesting piece of furniture. Even if the focal point is the television, you can make it beautiful in how you address it. Also remember that the view to the focal point should be unobstructed and not blocked visually by any piece of furniture. That means you can place a lower object within the space between the seating and the focal point, such as an ottoman or coffee table, but not a tall item.

After you have placed the largest pieces of furniture on the drawing of your room, add the remaining pieces of furniture according to their sizes, placing the smallest pieces last. As we previously discussed, a floor plan can be symmetrical or asymmetrical—but it must be in balance.

Asymmetrical is more casual and flexible. Symmetrical is more formal. To create balance, the large pieces should be evenly distributed. The easiest way to visualize this is to hold the drawing of your plan in the palm of your hand and imagine the weight distribution. Does the furniture look heavier on one side of the room, seeming to tilt to one side? If so, it's not balanced properly. Remember you can address balance either physically or optically.

I also recommend that you leave a little space around each of the larger items so they don't look crowded. Large pieces that are crammed into a space look uncomfortable. If

they look uncomfortable, people using the room will feel uncomfortable. It will feel cramped. Rooms need breathing spaces. You don't have to fill every nook and cranny. Accessories and artwork displayed sparingly make a room feel larger. A lot of little things can make even a large place feel small.

When I am selecting furniture for a room, I keep in mind the architectural shapes of the room. For example, a room with all linear details would seem out of balance if I simply added an S curve–shaped sofa into it. However, to echo the curve of a bay window, a curved sectional would be pleasing to the eye and would in fact make furniture arranging much easier.

When deciding on your furniture arrangement, keep in mind how the light affects appearances. A dark cabinet might disappear in a dimly lit corner. That can be good if the cabinet is not

**BELOW** To create unity within your home, decorate adjoining spaces in complementary colors and styles. (Photographer: Patty Minnick; room courtesy of Charter Homes and Neighborhoods, Lancaster, Penn.)

your favorite or if you think it might be a bit too large for the space. In that case, diminishing its appearance by placing it in a darker corner makes sense. But it can be bad if this is your focal piece of furniture. You might want to consider highlighting such a piece with additional lighting to bring it into view, or consider placing a lighter colored item in the dark corner instead. As a focal point, you would want to place the dark cabinet in the best light, which you can do by moving it or adding light fixtures to highlight it. Brightly colored items can seem garish in bright sunlight.

Take lighting into consideration as you create the floor plan for your room. I love brightly colored pillows, but changes in light can really alter their perceived colorations. One way I solve this dilemma in my very sunny family room is to use pillows with a different color on each side. During the light of day, I display the more subtly colored side. In the evening, I turn the pillows around to the brighter side.

As you are thinking about your floor plan, remember that you want to break up the horizontal lines of the room by mixing in taller items with shorter ones. You don't want your furniture to look like a train all lined up around the room. A bookcase or secretary placed against the wall with a chair or sofa or a pair of lamps on a credenza will give the eye variety and improve the overall view. Wall accessories can easily help in creating this variety when none would exist otherwise.

The room arrangement should make your desired activities comfortable and convenient as well as be flattering to the room. If you generally eat or drink in your family room, this should be a consideration when designing the floor plan. Make sure that you have adequate and easily reachable surfaces for setting down a cup or plate. Consider whether you have enough storage for books or CDs. Is the room plan conducive to socializing? Is there enough seating? My family room has seating for seven. But I can easily bring in an extra chair or bench from the adjoining rooms when necessary. By keeping a simple open floor plan, I have designed the space to be flexible.

## APPLY THE PLAN

This is a good time to reassess how your plan is coming together. Unless you are very visual and easily can imagine the drawn plan, then I would suggest rearranging your existing furniture to match the drawn plan. It's the best way to see how it feels. If you haven't yet purchased your new furniture, then cut out life-sized templates from newspaper or combine smaller pieces of furniture to create the size you need to represent the drawing. If you are like my hubby and find change difficult, give yourself several days to get used to the new ideas. I have a rule with clients: I will not take calls from them within the first twenty-four hours of delivering their new room. Why? Because no matter how perfect something is, most people panic at the initial change. It takes time to adjust.

Part of your assessment should be to consider your family and the way you like to live. If you have children or pets that like to roll around or sit on the floor, leave open space for them on the floor plan. Also, if your room is small in scale, consider fooling the eye by placing your sofa on the diagonal of a corner. This creates the optical illusion of more space. You can add a triangular table behind for accessories or a plant. The idea is to keep the visual depth of the corner while fooling the eye.

Also look at the vertical plan of your room.

Remember, when we talk about balance, not just the floor plan but also the elevations or wall plans must be equalized. Consider each wall individually. If your ceiling height is short, place objects high on the wall to keep the eye moving upward. Taller rooms can be brought into visual balance by placing something at the 8- or 9-foot height to give the eye a resting spot. Once you have addressed the primary functions and oriented the furniture around the focal point, it's time to add accent pieces and secondary activities. Floor plans that include secondary uses add to the functionality of a room. A reading corner in a bedroom is a good example.

Is there an empty space on your floor plan? Perhaps a blank wall? If you have as little as 12 inches of depth to work with, you can create a visually appealing accent while also providing additional function. In 12 inches of space you can add a bookcase, a bench, or even a beautiful hand-painted accent chest. You can then create a secondary focal point by grouping pictures above it. In my bedroom, I built a bookcase in the 12 inches of depth that I had. By taking it to the ceiling, I keep the eye moving upward, giving the appearance of more volume in the space.

As you consider locations for your furniture, keep in mind that items like to be related. In other words, two pieces of furniture placed next to each other should have a relationship. An end table placed next to a bookcase doesn't make sense. They have no inherent relationship to each other. However, an end table placed next to a chair or sofa does make relational sense.

I have a relational issue in my family room and it's all my husband's fault. You see, he likes to sit directly in front of the television. This is the spot where I placed the chaise lounge (in front of the window). The problem is that no

one makes a chaise long enough for him. So I purchased the longest one I could find along with a matching ottoman. By placing the ottoman at the foot of the chaise, it easily accommodates his long legs. However, the ottoman looks silly at the foot of the chaise because it doesn't make relational sense. So when he is not seated on the chaise, we move the ottoman into the corner and angle it on the diagonal where it looks terrific. I just turn a blind eye to the combination when he's using it.

Other ideas for accents and additional functions can include a desk placed at a window. A screen divider placed in a corner will soften it and add character while making the room feel cozy. I chose an antiqued mirror-finished floor screen for an empty corner in my living room. It created the perfect backdrop for an accent table and chair. My husband immediately commented on how cozy it looked. A corner cupboard or curio can be functional as well as provide display room for your favorite collection. Accent pieces should be in keeping with the overall style of the room, and add a fluid and integrated feel.

Remember to be aware of traffic patterns. You can actually direct traffic by the placement of furniture. I prefer to direct traffic around the perimeters of the room, to avoid interrupting

**OPPOSITE** A chair and ottoman, small table, basket of books, and warm throw transform a tiny corner into a cozy nook for reading. (Photographer: Patty Minnick; Interior Designer: Sharon Hanby-Robie)

**BELOW** Comfort is the priority when it comes to seating my tall husband. The cute little ottoman in the far right corner moves to the front of the chaise when he relaxes his long legs. (Photographer: Lynn Noble; Interior Designer: Sharon Hanby-Robie)

conversational groupings. If possible, leave a minimum of 2½ feet (30 inches) for walkways. Be consciously aware of the adjoining rooms as you determine which routes are best for traffic. Obviously, you want to create an easy traffic route to those adjoining rooms that are most often used. My kitchen directly adjoins my family room via a 5-foot opening. The flooring changes at that point from carpeting to resilient flooring. That visually helped to define the spaces. In laying out my rooms I made sure that traffic could easily flow from the foyer to the family room to the kitchen without obstruction.

Speaking of obstructions, some furniture styles and details create more visual obstruction than others. For example, when sofas and chairs are elevated on legs, it makes them appear lighter because you can see through them to the next view—even if it's just the wall beyond. It allows for greater depth perception. Anything heavy, such as a skirted table, will block

the eye movement through the space. A combi-nation of open leg and solid-to-the-floor items can help a room appear balanced.

Ultimately your floor plan should allow your room to be welcoming, open, reasonably neat, and comfortable, as well as visually appealing. Every room should have an element of surprise, so plan for that as well. The best-designed rooms are those that allow themselves to be reinvented to suit any occasion.

## NOW DO IT YOURSELF

■ **Take the time to draw out your room on paper.** It's the easiest way to give yourself an opportu-nity to see your room as a blank slate.

■ **Try out your new ideas for a floor plan by re-arranging your existing furniture to see how it feels.** Give yourself a week or two to adjust to the new placement. Remember, even a good change can take some time to get used to.

## STEP 4: Too Small? Too Tall? Too Many Windows?

In the previous step we discussed the basic floor plan. But many rooms have challenges that make creating an ideal plan difficult. I will attempt to address some of those issues, such as small rooms, tall rooms, rooms without walls, and rooms with odd shapes and angles. It will be impossible to address every odd room, but I will give you general principles for handling some specific issues, which you can apply to your situation.

Small rooms can pose the toughest decorating challenges. As I have said briefly before, one of the biggest misconceptions is thinking that small rooms need small-scale furniture, patterns, and so on to work—when in reality the opposite is true. Small-scale furniture shrinks the room even further. You may be able to fit in more pieces of smaller furniture, but they will only create visual clutter that makes the room feel smaller. Don't be afraid of large-scale furniture. Instead of small stuff, I recommend a few dramatic pieces such as a large armoire, a hutch, or comfy chairs. The larger scale fools the eye into believing the space is larger. This works because it doesn't clutter a room.

However, fewer items are definitely better in

**OPPOSITE** This light and airy room maintains its feel with furnishings that sit above the floor and allow breathing room beneath. (Photographer: Patty Minnick; room courtesy of Charter Homes and Neighborhoods, Lancaster, Penn.)

**BELOW** To accommodate additional seating in this compact family room, we added two storage ottomans that double as seating or a cocktail table. Using similar colors throughout also helped visually expand the space. (Photographer: Patty Minnick; Interior Designer: Sharon Hanby-Robie)

a small space. Paring down quantity and keeping the room from being crowded works best. When choosing furniture for a small room, it is incredibly important to determine exactly what you need rather than simply buying furniture to fill the room. Plan how much seating you realistically need for your family and your typical entertaining style. Then create your floor plan to accommodate just that and no more. Resist filling all the floor space. Instead work toward keeping the floor space open and as free as possible. Use furniture that you can see through. That doesn't mean that everything should be glass or Plexiglas, but do consider keeping an open airy feel under as much of the furnishings as possible. And always choose at least one tall element to extend the view upward into the otherwise uncrowded space above. This can be a piece of furniture, a piece of artwork, or even a beautiful chandelier. Another tip in choosing furnishings for smaller rooms is to take advantage of softer shapes. A round table takes up less space than a square table and adds a soothing softness at the same time.

The goal in small spaces is to always keep the eye moving out and beyond as much as possible, rather than resting or hitting on a wall. That's why it is important to take advantage of any view that your room has to offer, whether it's a view out the window or patio doors or simply a view of adjoining spaces. You can draw your eye out and into those adjoining spaces by using key pieces. For one client with small rooms, we opened the doorways as much as possible to create an unobstructed view from room to room. Then we purposely arranged the living room furniture so that it faced the view of the hand-painted hutch on the back wall of the dining room. The hutch acted like a magnet

**ABOVE** The view to my kitchen from my living/family room was greatly improved when I chose upscale accessories and artwork for the shelves and countertop in my kitchen. (Photographer: Lynn Noble; Interior Designer: Sharon Hanby-Robie)

**OPPOSITE** In small rooms, take advantage of vertical spaces by using built-ins. In this family room good planning helped gain enough space to add a fireplace. (Photographer: Patty Minnick; room courtesy of Steven L. Edris, Builder, Lancaster, Penn.)

for your eyes and drew you out and beyond the tiny living room, which made the living room feel much larger.

Always try your ideas for a floor plan by simply placing a chair in the space you are considering for your main seating pieces. My family room allows for only one place to position my sofa. One of the major views from the sofa is the kitchen: not my preference, but that is reality. So I improved the view with beautiful accessories on the kitchen counter and the shelf above. That viewpoint is critical to how the family room décor feels. If from that vantage point I were to simply see standard kitchen supplies, it would make the family room feel less formal and like part of the kitchen. But by purposely choosing extraordinary accessories for the kitchen that were in keeping with the family room décor, both rooms were enhanced.

Whenever I am working on a small room I have found that built-ins are invaluable. They allow you to use all the vertical space for abundant storage while only using a very small sec-

tion of floor space. Built-ins also give you an opportunity to add character to an otherwise unadorned setting. If carefully designed, they can perform multiple duties. A built-in bookcase can not only hold books and accessories, but also serve as an entertainment center.

Rooms with average or shorter ceiling heights benefit when we draw the eye upward. Start at the ceiling; the ceiling is the fifth wall of your room. Crown molding and ceiling details will automatically draw your eye upward and add the feeling of more volume to the room. In small spaces you can use this fifth wall to continue the visual expansion simply by using the same

color on it as you used on your walls. If you have used a faux painting technique or wallpaper on your walls, then continue it on the ceiling. The same technique is perfect for rooms with oddly angled walls or ceilings. Camouflaging these oddities by unifying them with color and treatment pushes them out and makes even the tiniest of spaces seem larger.

In rooms with 8-foot or shorter ceilings, I hang draperies as close to the ceiling as I can to continue that illusion of volume and expanding height. Simple window treatments are also critical for small spaces. Fussy, overdone drapery treatments can overwhelm and draw too much attention to themselves and away from the rest of your carefully planned room.

Choose a simple treatment that filters light while still allowing the benefit of filtered sun and privacy. Be sure that the color blends with your furnishings rather than contrasts. This will let you add texture and detail without chopping the wall visually into smaller pieces. If at all possible, extend the draperies beyond the window frame to give the illusion of a larger window. This too will help expand the overall impression of a small space. Simple side panels over a filtering shade are perfect. You can add details with trim and large-scale finials on your drapery rod. Again, choose colors that blend rather than contrast.

Overwhelming a small space with pattern is easy to do. Again, it may seem illogical, but small patterns with strong definition and contrast make small spaces look smaller. By using a large-scale pattern either on the walls or the upholstery, you visually enlarge the room. But avoid using too many patterns because it will confuse the eye. By using subtle patterns such as a tone-on-tone floral or stripe, you allow the eye to travel from one area to another without being interrupted by a jarring swath of color and pattern.

One of the most important elements to consider in a small room is color. Always opt for lighter-colored upholstery fabrics to unify your furniture and to expand small spaces. The rule of color says that pale tones advance, thus expanding spaces, while dark colors recede and thereby shrink a space. Creating a light and airy atmosphere is a key to making small spaces feel larger.

That's why it is important to keep your wall color a similar hue to your furnishings. This will help each piece of furniture blend seamlessly into the background rather than creating a dramatic contrast that cuts the room into smaller sections. Whenever you use loud or contrasting colors in a small space, the walls seem to close in on you. When choosing your wood or furniture for a small space, select lighter color wood tones or a painted piece that blends into the overall color scheme. Monochromatic (one-color) or two-color schemes work well in keeping visual simplicity and expanding a small space.

When it comes to accessories, one of the simplest ways to expand a small room is to keep clutter to a minimum. Another trick is to fool the eye by purposely not hanging artwork on center. Instead, hang it off center to make the eye focus on something other than the size of

the space. Artwork placed off center fools the eye because we assume it is centered, thereby enlarging the space of the wall. Also when two pieces of artwork are stacked, one on top of the other, it draws the eye up and creates volume. In small spaces, keep throw pillows to a minimum. Choosing a few larger pillows will gain volume, while several smaller ones will not.

## WHEN YOUR ROOM IS TOO TALL

A problem of rooms being too tall has arisen over the past three decades. At first, we all thought that these new soaring ceilings were fabulous. But it didn't take us long to realize that not only do they feel uncomfortable, but they are difficult to paint and decorate. Rooms that are too cavernous simply feel cold, not cozy. Bringing a too-tall room down to size is critical

**OPPOSITE** A monochromatic color palette infused with textures and subtle patterns unifies this small bedroom to create an airy but interesting atmosphere. (Photographer: Lynn Noble; Interior Designer: Gail Dunn)

**RIGHT** In this not so large, but tall dining room, the gold leaf finish on the ceiling not only gives the room a rich glow, but also helps to bring the room into proportion. (Photographer: Patty Minnick; Interior Designer: Sharon Hanby-Robie)

to making it feel inviting and functional. The first thing that must be tackled in a too-tall room is adding some visual weight. That means we need to once again fool the eye—this time into believing that the ceiling is lower than it is so that the room feels in proportion.

There are several ways to accomplish this. The easiest is simply to paint the ceiling a darker color. This will instantly add visual weight, thereby making it appear closer. If you have a trayed ceiling (resembling an upside-down tray), you can simply paint the interior portion a darker color. However, for a vaulted

ceiling (angled upward on one or both sides to create volume), I would recommend adding a few details and other visual definition. By adding molding around the walls you define and separate the ceiling from the walls.

The best way to add moldings is to choose a horizontal architectural feature as a reference

**BELOW** This light and airy room offers the best of all worlds. The strategic use of a soffit along a kitchen wall gives this side of the room the cozy Colonial feel that a period home should have. Yet the higher ceilings bring the room into the twenty-first century. (Photographer: Patty Minnick; room courtesy of Steven L. Edris, Builder, Lancaster, Penn.)

point for their position. You can either follow the horizontal line created by the top of the window frames or a transom, or choose a height that makes sense for your room. For one client, we used the line of the balcony railing as our designated spot for installing molding. When you paint all the area above the molding a darker color and paint all the surface area below a different but lighter color, the eye senses the difference. It assumes the room's ceiling or "lid" is at that new horizontal designation, which makes the walls feel shorter.

Another option is to add a shelf around the entire room at an 8- or 9-foot height. This is what I did in my powder room. This small room is 9 feet tall. The height was so out of proportion that it made the room feel much smaller than it is, so I installed a shelf at the height of 7 feet. I painted all the area above the shelf the darker color and used wallpaper below. This contrast and horizontal line designation instantly made the room feel well proportioned. Soffits are another good idea for taming too-tall rooms. A soffit is an underhang on the ceiling formed by the underside of an architectural element such as an arch, a staircase, or a projecting cornice. To make a room more inviting, you can install a soffit by lowering a narrow section of ceiling. The soffit not only gives the eye a visual stopping point, but helps organize larger spaces. Most soffits are 2 to 3 feet deep. I have a client with a very large kitchen/family room with high ceilings. I designed a soffit to follow the shape and size of the large kitchen island. Now that area feels defined and the visual lowering of the ceiling makes it feel cozier.

Of course, don't forget that you can always add visual interest to the vertical center of tall walls by giving your eye something to focus on.

By positioning a grouping of large pictures on the middle of the wall, you create a visual marker that keeps the eye from moving up the wall. Scale is critical. A series of large-scale pieces of artwork is best for tall spaces. Small ones will not work.

Don't be afraid to get creative and add dimension to your artwork on the wall. In one home I used a custom piece of artwork that was sculpted out of heavy art paper. It was about 6 feet in diameter and nearly 16 inches deep. As I was positioning it at the 9- to 10-foot height on the wall, the depth was not a problem. This sculpture became a secondary focal point and filled an otherwise vast void of space (the ceiling height was 21 feet). Because of the location of the wall, I could not place furniture against it. The artwork was the perfect solution.

## WHEN THE ROOM SEEMS TOO OPEN

Open floor plans can also be difficult spaces to manage. We love the fact that they give us greater flexibility for entertaining and daily living. We love the abundance of daylight that they allow. But we struggle with creating boundaries and defining spaces. And these areas can be very noisy. Sounds are magnified by the tall ceiling surfaces. Even in my own home, the open loft from the second floor acts like a microphone for every noise downstairs. Simply making a cup of coffee in the morning can wake everyone in the entire house. I can't solve all these problems, especially the noise issue, but some things can be done to help make sense out of such vast spaces and turn the volume down a notch or two.

Architecturally, we can vary the height of ceilings to create intimacy and distinction between different activity areas. For example,

help soften and contain noise. Area rugs also define spaces.

Even if you can't change the height of your actual ceilings, you can create the illusion of a lower ceiling by hanging accessories from the ceiling. Pendant lamps hung over a table or corner create such an illusion. For one client, we built a beautiful open grid of wood and hung it by chains from the ceiling over the main living area. This gave that section of the room a "lid" that brought the room into proportion while adding warmth and detail at the same time. Another way to define spaces within an open floor plan is to simply change the finish material on ceilings. Wood planked ceilings are becoming more and more popular and are easily installed on an existing ceiling finish.

Changes to the flooring also are an easy way to define unique spaces in an open area. They naturally create boundaries from one room to another. Even if you choose to use hardwood or other hard-surface flooring throughout your home, you can add rugs to give a foundation to specific areas. To define rooms within an open floor plan, I love using wall-to-wall rugs that have been cut to a specific size and bound to create a finished edge. It's a great way to define space without being forced to make a significant statement with pattern and color. Of course, in

in my kitchen, most of the ceiling is 9 feet tall. However, in the breakfast nook area, the ceiling soars into a vaulted height with two skylights. This distinction sets this portion of the room apart, making it feel special and different from the rest of the kitchen. Changes in ceiling height will also help reduce the magnification of sounds. Of course, adding sound-absorbing materials to your decorating plans will also make a difference in noise levels. Area rugs and upholstered furnishings definitely

large open spaces you can always choose the bolder fashion statement of area rugs. But often I have found I need a larger or more square rug, so wall-to-wall cut to size is simpler.

## NOW DO IT YOURSELF

■ **Evaluate the height of your room.** If it feels too tall, then consider artwork, molding, or other eye-attracting methods to bring it down to size. If it's too short, consider painting the ceiling and walls all the same color to create the illusion of never-ending space.

## STEP 5: Taking the Basement to a New Level

When I was a child, the basement was the place where we children could get rowdy without a reprimand. We could run, hide, play, or even argue without our parents telling us to use our "inside" voices. It was the best place in the house. As we grew into teenagers, this space became even more important. We were the fortunate beneficiaries of the basement recreation room that our father built from plans in magazines

such as *Popular Mechanics.* Soundproof and relatively private, this room was a place where we could listen to music and socialize without parental interference. As *Better Homes and Gardens* writer Curtiss Anderson observed in 1954, the basement provided a multipurpose space: "People live in basements. Women do laundry in basements. Children play in basements. Handymen work in basements. Families have parties in basements. Scooters and screens, furniture and food, tools and toys, and boxes and bicycles are stored in basements."

Then somewhere around the 1970s a new and supposedly brilliant idea took hold: We started building family rooms. These spaces were supposed to be ideal because they were above ground level and promoted family togetherness. In theory this sounded great, but in reality, I think parents and children benefit from some separateness. And as trends usually follow our desires, over the past ten years or so,

the family recreation room has returned. And it's better than ever. It's no longer the dark, cold, black hole of previous generations. Some of today's basement recreation rooms are worthy of publication in prestigious magazines.

And these rooms are paying off in value too. According to *Remodeling Magazine*'s Cost vs. Value Report, the average basement remodel now includes a 20 by 30-foot entertaining area with wet bar, a 5 by 8-foot full bath, and a 12 by 12-foot auxiliary room. The average cost for such a space is now $43,112. And according to real estate agents and appraisers, the average expected return is 79 percent or $33,911. That's an impressive return on investment, especially when you consider the value it brings to your everyday life.

The good news about remodeling a basement is that you already own the space. Therefore, it will be much less expensive to finish a basement than to build an addition to your house. The average cost per square foot to finish a basement is less than half of that for an addition. But there are challenges to spaces below ground. Some of the inherent challenges you will face are low ceilings, dampness, and poor lighting. But these are not insurmountable, and with a few pointers you too can take your basement living to a whole new level. Your basement can be transformed into the room of your dreams.

## SO LET'S DIG IN

As with all rooms, it's best to start by simply assessing your needs. Do you need a home office? An extra bedroom? A place to exercise? Or simply a place to send your teenagers?

Next it's time to consider what is required to fulfill those needs. For example, will you need to add insulation to muffle the sounds of your teens and all their friends? How about a mini-kitchen or a bathroom? When I finished my basement, I added a full bath and planned for a kitchenette. I also left enough room for storage. Finishing off a basement will rob you of all its open storage area. If you don't make plans for storage, you will find your new space housing an array of items that don't necessarily go with your new décor. It's also a good idea to plan for years to come and design spaces that will be adaptable for the future. If you are considering a bedroom in your basement, check with your local zoning board about zoning and code requirements for such a use.

One of your first considerations when it comes to creating a floor plan for a basement is the location of bathrooms and kitchenettes.

Bathrooms located lower than the service lines for the rest of the house will usually require installing an ejector pump in the floor. Consult a plumber early on to help you locate the most economical position for such an installation.

The best floor plans in basements result from establishing different zones within the overall *open* plan. You want to be able to capture as much light and air movement as possible. So I

**OPPOSITE**  Color-saturated chairs are functional art that helped transform a basement into a vibrant design. (Photographer: Lori Stahl; Interior Designer: Sharon Hanby-Robie)

**BELOW**  This billiard hall–inspired recreation room easily accommodates fun and food with the addition of a practical kitchenette. (Photographer: Patty Minnick; room courtesy of Charter Homes and Neighborhoods, Lancaster, Penn.)

don't recommend using full walls to create your zones. Instead, half walls, glass block walls, and changes in flooring can help delineate different zones. Of course, most basements also have structural elements, such as support columns and pipe runs, that must be considered.

Basement ceilings are generally lower than other areas of your house, so making accommodations for ducts, pipes, and electrical work that fit your ideal layout can be tricky. If at all possible, incorporate the space needed to house these necessities into your plan. For example, you can use the soffits needed for these items to your advantage by placing elements under them that make sense. A counter or bar that follows the lines of the soffit can fit beautifully. You can also add columns that look like they are part of the structural and design continuity. A lower ceiling section is also the perfect place to designate a change in zones. One side can be for movie viewing, and the other for game tables, with a cabinet between that allows for abundant storage.

## DEAL WITH THE MOISTURE

All the planning in the world can be wasted if you don't first drive out the dampness. Temperature and ventilation can help keep humidity under control, but many older basements also need a dehumidifier to help dispel moisture and improve circulation. I also recommend installing an automatic sump pump. The installation of an air exchange system vented to the outdoors can help alleviate moisture and stagnant air, which promotes mold and mildew. Water is a persistent problem that can be difficult to fix after you have remodeled. Assessing your dampness situation and taking steps to prevent it will save you money and frustration later.

Some of the telltale signs to look for are subflooring leaks. Fix any faulty pipes and fixtures first. Brownish stains on the basement subfloor and sides of the basement joists can indicate an active or an old leak. If it's spongy—it's active.

## ADD SOME LIGHT

I am fortunate because I have a walkout basement that includes patio doors and two windows. But even so, I worked the plan to encourage natural light to extend far into the interior spaces. You too should capitalize on any source of available daylight, no matter how small. It's as simple as positioning openings and hallways so that window light extends as far into the interior as possible.

Window wells have become increasingly important as we finish basements. As a result, they are now designed to be better looking and to easily provide the necessary egress (exit) that most communities require. For example, the ScapeWEL provides a terraced step design that aids in emergency escapes. These terraced steps also provide planting space to visually enhance the well. But best of all, this window well allows more natural light into the basement and comes in colors that complement most interiors. To see it, visit www.bilco.com and search for ScapeWEL.

Lighting is probably the most critical element when it comes to planning a basement remodel. Whenever I am reviewing a contractor's bid for a basement remodel, I warn the client to expect to double the electrical budget suggested because it almost always is not enough to do the job correctly. The best approach to properly lighting a basement is a multiple one. By blending a variety of light sources you can create a comfortable, well-lit

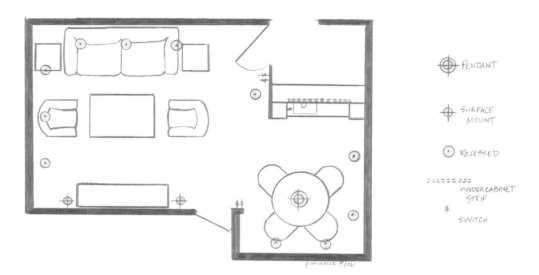

PENDANT

SURFACE MOUNT

RECESSED

UNDER CABINET STRIP

SWITCH

p.mindick 9/06

lower living area. Mixing table lamps with recessed fixtures, pendant lamps, and sconces can illuminate a basement to accommodate activities any time of day or evening. All lighting plans should include ambient and task lighting. These should correspond to the zoned areas of activity. Recessed lights should be placed no more than 6 to 8 feet apart for efficiency. You can also create false windows that include back-lighting. You won't get a lot of light from them, but the ambiance and the illusion they bring helps you feel above ground rather than below.

### CREATE AN ENTRANCE

One of the latest trends for basements is to eliminate the basement door and open the stairway into the rest of the home. Using simi-lar architectural details throughout connects the basement to the rest of the house. I love the

**ABOVE** A well-lit room requires layers of light. This lighting plan shows how a variety of fixtures and lamp styles can light up a basement room. (Illustrator: Patty Minnick)

way this looks. But you must decide how much quiet and privacy you need. I know, for me, even with my basement office door closed I can still be distracted by activities going on above. Being able to close the basement door makes a world of difference for me. This problem could be solved, however, by placing a door at the bottom of the stair instead.

In my particular situation, an open stairway is not an option, but it is something you should consider when making your plan. Recognize also that if you choose to create an open stair-way and repeat architectural details for conti-nuity—such as matching moldings and trim, door styles and hardware—this will cost more than choosing less expensive elements. Make your choices based on how you want to use the space. If this will simply be a place for teens, crafts, and storage, I probably wouldn't invest in the extras. However, if you plan on adding a home theater and major entertaining area, then it could be worth the investment.

As you are analyzing your basement plan, note all its nooks and crannies. This will be helpful for positioning built-ins and storage. Recently, I was asked to do a walk-through of a client's basement just as the first sections of framing had been installed in their soon-to-be-finished basement rec room. While walking through the half-finished space, we discovered hidden spaces that might have been inaccessible when finished. By simply adding access

doors, we gained an incredible amount of storage. We were also able to purposely place cabinetry in a recess rather than extend it out into the room. This saved just enough space to add a pool table that otherwise might not have fit.

This near-miss in my client's basement remodel happened because the contractor drew the original plans to keep costs low. As a result, he had not budgeted for the additional framing of nooks, crannies, and niches. I am sure that he did this to help lower his bid so he could get the job. However, if he had taken the time to truly understand the client's desires and willingness to spend what was necessary, he could have done a far better job and made the client much happier in the end. That's what careful planning is all about.

## ALWAYS PLAN FOR FUTURE ADAPTATIONS

When planning for remodels, I always take the client to the highest level of expectation. We can always work our way down but at least I

**BELOW** The excellent lighting and wonderful textures in this basement family room make it the perfect environment for family and friends. (Photographer: Lynn Noble)

know that we have pursued all the options. A desperately needed pantry can be built in a small recessed area, or better yet, a full walk-in closet or wine cellar can be added. Foresight is always better than hindsight in building projects.

Whenever a client initiates a remodeling project, I ask him or her to consider adaptable designs. Eighty-five percent of us want to remain in our homes as we age. Adaptable design, also referred to as accessible or universal design, ensures that the space will successfully meet a broad set of needs. We used to think that only the handicapped benefited from such designs. The reality is all of us benefit in the long run. As we age, our needs change. For example, the older we get, the more light we need. By taking this into account when remodeling, you can provide abundant light and ample maneuvering space. Or you could leave room to accommodate an elevator or chairlift later. Even if it is never installed, it is reassuring to know that you can do it without major renovation.

Other considerations for adaptable design include easy access for a wheelchair or walker. By planning for a larger open area under a desk, craft, or sink counter, you make the space accessible to a wheelchair. In bathrooms, grab bars are helpful for everyone and reduce the risk of falling. One of my clients had broken his back and to reassure him, we rearranged the floor plan to have something every few feet he could grab onto for balance and stability. Part of that plan involved adding railings to walls. It was simple and effective.

# NOW DO IT YOURSELF

- **Plan for long-term flexibility**. When I was planning to finish my basement, I knew that I needed office and storage space. However, I also took into consideration that the next owners might prefer to use this space for a recreation room and perhaps an additional bedroom or two. I deliberately devised a plan that can easily be adapted later to accommodate teenage children or in-laws with very little effort. The layout of the space in my basement can easily allow for those situations as well as my own.

- **Consider your options well when choosing flooring.** If you choose a durable surface, you can easily add an area rug to soften and define specific areas within your plan. An easy-to-install electric floor heating system can make your basement a much more comfortable environment. Warmly Yours (www.WarmlyYours.com) has two different systems available: one for hard flooring such as stone, tile, or hardwood; and another for soft flooring such as carpeting or floating wood floor systems like laminate floors or prefinished wood flooring systems.

# CHAPTER 5

# Let There Be Light

- ■ **STEP 1: DAYLIGHT MATTERS**
- ■ **STEP 2: THREE LAYERS OF LIGHT**

**H**enry David Thoreau shed a little light on the subject of design when he wrote, "Always the laws of light are the same, but the modes and degrees of seeing vary." I love this quotation because it shows just how important and how complex light really is. And light is so important to the overall appearance of every item within your home. As the light of day changes, shadows move and change color as well. Our goal is to find the perfect light for painting the most beautiful spaces.

# STEP 1: Daylight Matters

Sunlight is by far the most important source of light and energy for living organisms. Most of us spend part of our day under the influence of sunlight. Sadly, however, as an urbanized society we are spending less and less time outdoors, which means much of the light that we live under is not natural. And that's a problem—natural light not only gives the best color rendition, but is essential to our health and well-being.

Tom Wehr, MD, a research psychiatrist at the National Institutes of Health and an expert in mood disorders, believes that our elevation in mood during the spring and summer can be directly linked to the amount of sunlight we are exposed to. Exposure to natural light increases production of serotonin, which elevates mood and helps ward off depression, says Dr. Wehr in an article in the online resource YourSkinAndSun.com. "Besides just making us feel better and more energetic, exposure to sunlight plays an important role in helping us create vitamin D in our bodies." Vitamin D has many health benefits, including helping maintain strong bones.

The reality is that daylight has a huge effect not only on how we feel, but also on how we feel about our homes in general. As our homes have evolved to bigger and more open floor plans, many of the activities have moved away from the perimeter walls toward the center and away from natural light. If bringing daylight further into the home can elevate our moods, create more welcoming spaces, and save on energy bills, why wouldn't we do our best to accomplish this? Part of the problem, as I have discussed earlier, is that often windows are simply placed in a position that makes the exterior look good—without considering the illumination or the architectural integrity of the interior.

As an interior designer, I am always struggling with how to best take advantage of the natural light of these badly placed windows, while attempting to create window treatments that control light and privacy, and complement the décor. This feat has become increasingly more difficult because the bigger the window, the bigger the issues and the more expensive the window treatment.

We all love natural light. So we thought adding more windows could make our homes feel better. That works to some degree, but at what cost? The large, architecturally designed detailed windows and the window treatments used to adorn them can be expensive. The goal should be to get the most light out of fewer windows and skylights and extend that light further into the home environment. The good news is that there are ways to enhance windows and skylights to make the most of daylight.

## CAPTURE REFLECTIVE LIGHT

One of the simplest methods is to create *reflection* of light. If you have ever seen a professional photographer or videographer working, you may have noticed a large silver or white board being moved about. This is a *reflector*. By moving it around you can actually capture natural light and reflect it onto the surface of the subject being photographed. It's used a lot in television, too. When we recently shot video of a kitchen renovation for QVC, we used several reflectors to balance the light around the room and eliminate dark corners.

This same theory can work with your own window light. Simply adding a shelf above a

window can create such a reflecting surface. The lighter you paint the underside of the shelf, the more reflection you will get. You can further enhance light from a window by building a bookcase alongside it. The side of the bookcase should also be a light color to gain the most reflection. The result will be a room that appears to have more daylight. One of my favorite design elements is to build a bookcase that surrounds an expanse of glass, whether windows or doors. If it's a bank of windows, I usually add a window seat as well. This adds yet another surface for reflecting more light into the room.

If you have the opportunity to choose where to put windows to gain the most light, place

**ABOVE** Painted in delicious contemporary colors, this kitchen is eclectically energetic. The decorative cornice above the window also helps reflect daylight. (Photographer: Lynn Noble; Interior Designer: Sharon Hanby-Robie)

them adjacent to surfaces that can act as reflectors. If you are going to place windows in the center of a wall, place them near the ceiling so the ceiling can act as a reflector. Or place them adjacent to a wall so the entire wall can be infused with light. This will give your room a wonderful soft glow without the need for artificial lighting during daylight hours.

When I was building my own home, I knew that I wanted to capture as much natural light as possible. I wanted to avoid using skylights if

I could, because they create a penetration through the roof, which can cause heat loss and increased energy bills. Any glass used, even triple-paned, has a lower resistance to heat flow than an insulated roof. Window heat loss can be controlled with the proper window treatment or shading from landscaping, but heat loss through skylights cannot be controlled.

That said, I was carefully watching the amount of light that was penetrating into the further recesses of the home throughout the building process. When they finally closed in the roof, I walked through the house and found two areas that would be too dark for my liking: the fam-ily room and the kitchen/dining nook. I added two skylights to each area. For me, it was the right decision. Those few skylights allow me to do without artificial lighting until the sun goes down. Everyone that comes to my home loves the way the natural light feels. It is bright and soothing.

## SWITCH BULBS TO IMPROVE YOUR DESIGN

Color is incredibly important to an interior designer. But the best of plans can turn into a color nightmare with the flick of a light switch. When I am selecting paint, fabric, and other finishes for color, I always work in natural light.

Then I take all the samples to the location where they will be used. Even a carefully chosen color palette can be ruined with the wrong type of light. The best-lit rooms are those that use layers of light from several different sources. But the key ingredient is the types of lamps (or bulbs) that are chosen.

There are two crucial factors for choosing a lightbulb. First is the color temperature or chromaticity. This refers to the perceived warmth or coolness. The scientific measurement for this is degrees *Kelvin:* The higher the degrees Kelvin, the cooler the light. Natural daylight is about 5500 degrees Kelvin. The second crucial factor is the color rendering index, or *CRI*. This is a number between 1 and 100. The higher the CRI, the better colors appear. Natural daylight has a CRI of 100. It offers exceptional color rendering. Although daylight's chromaticity fluctuates, in general, it is slightly "cool."

The normal household lightbulb is the most familiar incandescent light. But it is not the only incandescent lamp. In fact, there are hundreds. For example, GE's Reveal bulbs make colors "pop" in a way they don't with standard incandescent bulbs. It's the rare element neodymium in the glass of these bulbs that makes the difference and gives them a distinctive blue color when unlit. All incandescent bulbs have a dull yellow cast when lit, but the neodymium in the Reveal bulbs provides a pure, clean light by filtering out much of the yellow. It's not quite as nice as natural sunlight, but it's closer than a standard incandescent bulb.

Another incandescent bulb that many people are familiar with is the halogen lamp. The normal household lightbulb gives a warm wash of golden light, while the halogen lamp is slightly whiter. Halogen bulbs also burn hotter. All halogen light fixtures should have a shield around the bulb for protection. Also note that halogen bulbs should not be handled with bare hands. The oil from our hands causes the bulb to burn out. Use a soft cloth when changing a halogen bulb.

**OPPOSITE** The light from this wall of windows is increased by its reflection off adjacent walls, ceiling, and other surfaces. (Photographer: Lynn Noble; Interior Designer: Gail Dunn)

**LEFT** Every sunrise sheds light on my living/family room through windows and skylights. (Photographer: Lynn Noble; Interior Designer: Sharon Hanby-Robie)

Fluorescent lamps have had a bad rap for a long time. The good news is that this is changing. We like them because they use less energy and add less heat to a room. Designers hate them because they cast a dreaded harsh, greenish hue. But technology has improved dramatically and they now come in a variety of colors that do not cast that greenish hue. There are warm whites and cool blues. Warm fluorescents are great for enhancing colors in the red and yellow palette, while cool fluorescents make blues and greens pop!

CFLs (compact fluorescent lightbulbs) have been coming on strong. Anyone who is very energy conscious thinks they are fabulous. They cost as much as six dollars a bulb, but are supposed to last four to seven years. They are also better for the environment because they do not produce the carbon dioxide and sulfur that incandescent bulbs do. But most of us find CFLs to be a nuisance because they take a moment or two to come on. You flick the switch and wait . . . until finally you have light. But it's not as bright as you expected. And the light is harsh—too white. A new generation of CFLs is Energy Star-rated and said to be brighter and even more efficient. (They use less energy, save money, and help protect the environment.) A 15-watt CFL should produce the same brightness as a 60-watt incandescent. If you want more light, simply use a higher wattage CFL. You will still be saving money, while doing your part to help the environment.

And the latest development is a CFL enhancer called the PowerRim, which promises to boost the amount of illumination each CFL provides while reducing the heat it produces. It is also said to extend its longevity. But it's not cheap—about $100 for each enhancer.

One of the most recent light source developments is LEDs. Recently I had a laser treatment on my face to remove precancerous cells. I was not allowed to see the light of day, or any other type of light, especially fluorescent, for twenty-four hours. Of course my office is lit with fluorescent lamps. So my assistant, Patty, offered a solution that would allow me to read and write without exposing my face to light. It was a nifty "brim" light that attaches to a cap or visor and uses LED lamps. When my cat approached me, she cringed, and off she went to find comfort elsewhere. But it worked for my purposes. I have seen several flashlights that use LED light, and a few residential lamps designed specifically for LED—but most are desk lamps and other utility style lamps.

## A NOTE ABOUT HIGHLIGHTING

Now that you understand many of the options for light sources, let's talk about what happens to light as we begin to use it and point it at objects in your home. Let's start with a natural delight: the rainbow. When we look at a rainbow, we are actually seeing the wavelengths of the visible colors. As the sun emits its radiation in this visible range, our eyes interpret it as the colors of the rainbow. These colors are identified as the *visible spectrum* of red, orange, yellow, green, blue, indigo, and violet.

Light travels in the form of a wave. White light, or the light from the sun, is made of colors of light; each color has its own wavelength by which we identify that color. Waves also exist above and below our visible spectrum. Radio, microwave, and infrared are below the red end of the spectrum and ultraviolet (UV), X-rays, and gamma rays are above the violet.

When light waves travel they can be *reflected,*

**ABOVE**  Just the right light puts the focus on art. (Photographer: Lori Stahl; Interior Designer: Sharon Hanby-Robie)

*absorbed,* or *transmitted.* This is determined by the object the wave hits. If we perceive an object to be black, all the wavelengths of light hitting that object are being absorbed and no light is reflected. Most solid objects will reflect light. Obviously, transparent objects will allow light to transmit through them. All of this is taken into consideration as we begin to light a room and the objects within them. If we can plan for how light will react to the largest and most significant objects within a room, we can do a better job.

For example, I know I need to accommodate dark or near black tones with more light or more reflective surfaces to enhance the quality of light within the space. Or, for a more dramatic appeal, I might choose to highlight a few specific items within the room. Have you ever seen a theater production where the entire set is black except for the one person standing on stage? It takes as many as eight spotlights to create that effect. Now imagine trying to create a similar effect on a sculpture in a room. When I am working with clients, these are some of the considerations that I try to plan for. If a client has an extensive collection, we want it to be seen in the best light. But the composition of that collection brings with it unique characteristics that affect how I choose to light it. A solid dark object requires a different set of techniques than a glass collection, for example. I will address some of these topics in the next section (Step 2).

**NOW** DO IT YOURSELF

# STEP 2: Three Layers of Light

- Look for ways within your home to capture more natural daylight and draw it further into your room by adding a reflective shelf or bookcase around your windows.

- Improve how your room looks simply by changing your lightbulbs to full-spectrum or GE Reveal bulbs. If you are energy conscious, try one of the new CFL bulbs. You may find that seeing your room in a whole new light improves the way you feel too.

I often say, "If you ask ten different interior designers for an opinion about something, you will get ten different opinions." The reason is simple—we each have our own preferences and concepts of what constitutes good design. When you ask designers about lighting, the same principle holds true. We all believe in layering light in a room, but how and what effect we consider most desirable is debatable.

**OPPOSITE** The three layers of light in this Shaker style kitchen make it a glowing example of practical and beautiful. The downlights provide a combination of task and ambient lighting, the chandeliers provide accent lighting, and the under-cabinet lights provide task and ambient lighting. (Photographer: Patty Minnick; room courtesy of Steven L. Edris, Builder, Lancaster, Penn.)

**RIGHT** Accent lighting inside the glass door cabinet gives this corner a warm and wonderful glow. (Photographer: Patty Minnick; room courtesy of Steven L. Edris, Builder, Lancaster, Penn.)

I think that most of us strive to light spaces evenly to create an overall glow in the room, while eliminating dark corners as much as possible. Yet, some designers believe that an evenly lit room is boring. They believe the eye needs resting spaces. Ultimately, once again the right answer is in the eye of the beholder. The decision is yours.

Three basic types of lighting are required to properly light a room: *ambient, accent,* and *task.* Ambient light is the background level of light. It establishes the overall illumination to create an inviting atmosphere. It provides the greatest diffusion, or spreading out of light, to fill the entire space with a soft glow. This is accomplished by placing the lighting at the ceiling with either ceiling-mount fixtures or recessed cans. I always recommend that you use a dimmer for this portion of your lighting because it will allow you to create a variety of moods with a simple switch.

All light projects in the shape of a beam. A typical recessed 40-watt flood lamp placed 8 feet high will have a maximum beam spread of about 9 feet. The most intense light will be at the center (5 feet) and gradually decrease as you move out from the center. The height of your ceiling and the effect you desire will directly influence how many fixtures you use and where you place them. You may want to completely cover a wall with light, create an arched effect with light, or direct light toward artwork.

Most adjustable recessed cans have a maximum tilt of 35 degrees. Just as with natural light, we want to use the wall as a reflector to help create the desired effect. If your goal is to light artwork, and you have an 8-foot ceiling, your fixture would be placed about 20 inches away from the wall to light artwork placed at average viewing height, which is 63 inches from the floor. If your ceiling is 9 feet high, the proper distance to place the fixture is 27 inches from the wall. To best view artwork hung at average viewing height for a 10-foot ceiling, place the fixture about 33 inches from the wall.

Obviously the taller the ceiling, the more difficult it is to light artwork properly with an ambient fixture. To light artwork on a wall with rooms 12 feet or higher, I recommend fixtures that are specifically designed for situations like this, such as a fixture that is designed for a halogen lamp. I generally recommend that recessed lighting in a normal setting such as a family or living room be placed no more than 5 to 6 feet apart. If you want to wash your walls with light and create an evenly lit room, then the best plan would allow for the beams of light to overlap by placing more fixtures closer together, so that you have continuous light. (I'll talk about kitchens and bathrooms later in the section because they are more complicated.)

Accent lighting is exactly what it sounds like. It focuses the lighting on specific objects or areas within the room. It is used to emphasize what we find interesting in a room. It's also per-

fect for directing your eye to architectural features. The most effective method is using directional lighting: spotlights, track lights, cable lights, sconces, table lamps, or even a single-point halogen fixture. Ideally the light beam should cover the entire object, but only the object. If the beam is larger than the object, the light will spill onto walls and other surfaces and take the focus or emphasis off the object.

Chandeliers, pendants, and other decorative lamps are also considered accent lighting because they draw your eye to themselves. They become the lit feature. Accent light adds extra light and can create the illusion of a larger space when focused on the perimeter of a room. Our eye is always drawn to light. That is why when we walk into a room with a window, we usually see the window before we see the rest of the interior. By lighting the back wall of a room with accent lighting, you can give the illusion of a deeper space. The rule to remember with accent lighting is to use it sparingly, because it can cause sensory overload by leading the eye in too many directions.

Task lighting specifically illuminates work areas, such as countertops, islands, cooktops, and tables. Task lighting makes your life and work easier. A reading lamp placed next to your bed is a good example of a task light. In a kitchen, task lighting can be a recessed fixture or a series of lights placed under the wall cabinets in your kitchen to light the countertop. They can be halogen, puck light (a small, low-voltage disk that puts out a huge amount of pure-white light), incandescent strips, fluores-

cent tubes, or even rope lights. Remember, each of these provides a specific color of light and entails a different energy cost.

All rooms should include these three types of lighting. In my living room I have six recessed fixtures on a dimmer; one spotlight on a dimmer, shining on the fireplace mantel; a halogen floor lamp with two adjustable arms; and a table lamp. My room at the highest point of the vaulted ceiling is 20 feet high and is approximately 14 by 18 feet in dimension. The six recessed fixtures are on one switch, and the spotlight on another. This allows me to completely control the light for whatever mood I want to create. In my bedroom I have a spotlight over the bed to accent the wall behind it, two recessed fixtures for ambient light, a wall-mounted swivel-arm lamp for my husband to read by, and a table lamp on my nightstand. The room is 15 by 17 feet. The recessed fixtures are on one switch and the spotlight on another for flexibility. I also placed a switch at the bed to control all the lights for convenience.

## LIGHTING THE KITCHEN

Kitchens and bathrooms are the most complicated rooms to light properly because of the diversity of activities. A kitchen lighting plan should be functional as well as aesthetically pleasing. The three types of lighting often overlap. Recessed or track lighting makes a lot of sense for ambient light, but when placed to

**OPPOSITE** Eighteenth-century style chandeliers work their magic, but recessed ceiling fixtures make this kitchen a well-lit delight. (Photographer: Patty Minnick; room courtesy of Steven L. Edris, Builder, Lancaster, Penn.)

**LEFT** Pendant lighting adds that something extra, providing task lighting with an artistic flair. (Photographer: Lynn Noble)

**LEFT**  Perfectly suited for the period and style, this simple Shaker kitchen desk has the advantage of an under-cabinet light source that makes this space as beautiful as it is practical. (Photographer: Patty Minnick; room courtesy of Steven L. Edris, Builder, Lancaster, Penn.)

**OPPOSITE**  The beauty of this crystal chandelier sets the tone for an elegantly appealing atmosphere. (Photographer: Lori Stahl; Interior Designer: Sharon Hanby-Robie)

ceiling lights or desk lamps on each side of the task area to minimize glare and reflections. For tasks in which people are looking forward, such as computer work, it is important to locate downlights in front of the person to avoid casting unnatural and unpleasant shadows.

## HANGING THE CHANDELIER

One of the most asked questions that I hear is, "What height should I hang my chandelier?" Generally speaking, it should be 30 inches above the surface of your dining table to avoid interrupting sight lines. (You want to be able to see the face of the person sitting across from you.) This is also the correct position for pendant lamps hanging over an island or counter in a kitchen. However, don't be afraid to hang your chandelier a few inches lower if you like. The key is to let proportion and composition be your guide. Larger chandeliers fill up more space and feel more overwhelming when placed lower. Your overall composition should make sense to the height of your ceiling and other visual attractions within the room. It's like composing a painting or a photograph. What makes or breaks this composition is the size of the chandelier.

When selecting a chandelier, don't worry about the fixture's quality of light as much as its beauty and scale. (Remember, you should have

illuminate a countertop they act as task lights. Pendant lamps hung over an island act as ambient light as well as task lighting. Under-cabinet lights can illuminate a countertop (task lighting) while also accenting the tile backsplash.

Every work surface in a kitchen should be well illuminated with appropriate task lighting. You should strive to eliminate glare on countertops as much as possible. For counter or work surface tasks, recessed fixtures on the ceiling should be placed between the cabinet face and the front edge of the counter. This position avoids casting of shadows and minimizes reflections. When lighting areas for paper tasks like a kitchen desk, position downlights such as layers of light.) Think of your chandelier as more of a decorative accessory in the room. Chandelier choices include everything from exposed bulbs to large glass light-diffusing bowls. Style and finish should be the most important factors in choosing a chandelier that complements the rest of the room. Some of the more popular materials include brass, aluminum, wrought iron, other metal combinations, or composite materials. And crystal chandeliers are one of the most popular choices for a Traditional dining room setting. They create an ethereal, magical look, even when they are not turned on. One of the newer trends I am seeing is *candleliers*. These are candle-powered, nonelectric decorative lamps that are used as mood enhancers. It's a trend that goes back decades—antique chandeliers, of course, were not wired for electricity originally.

To find the right size chandelier for your room, choose one with a diameter that is 12 inches less than the width of your table. For ceilings 9 feet or higher, consider a two-tier chandelier to fill the space from the fixture's top to the ceiling. If you can't find a chandelier whose dimensions are perfect, err on the side of larger rather than smaller.

Today we are using chandeliers in almost any room: great rooms, foyers, bedrooms, powder rooms, and bathrooms. Choosing the right proportion for your room is critical for composing the perfect light. Here's how to determine the right size chandelier for your room: Multiply the width of your room in inches by 0.30 and the height of your room in inches by 0.25, and you'll have the approximate size of the chandelier.

Room width in inches x .30 =
width of chandelier in inches

Room height in inches x .25 =
height of chandelier in inches

Say your room is 12 feet wide and 16 feet high. That translates to 144 inches wide and 192 inches high. Now just multiply the width, 144 inches, by 0.30, and you will get 43.2 inches. Then multiply the height of 192 inches by 0.25, and you get 48 inches.

So your chandelier should measure approximately 44 inches wide by 50 inches tall. A chandelier of this size in a room with a 16-foot ceiling should be hung 10 feet from the floor.

## LIGHTING THE BATHROOM

Bathrooms are other spaces where we need to accommodate many different activities. We want lots of light in the morning so we can put our best face forward. But we also want to be able to create a sanctuary for relaxation in the evening. So the two most important types of light in a bathroom are ambient for the overall light in the room, and task for the vanity, shower, and tub areas. Again, I think that recessed fixtures make the most sense for ambient lighting. Of course, dimmers are the simplest way to provide flexibility. They allow you to set the light low for night and for relaxing in the tub. Also, remember to install separate switches to control ambient light and task lighting.

The finishes in a bathroom will affect your lighting plan, too. Your floor, ceiling, and wall finishes will either reflect light or absorb light. If you want to use dark, dramatic colors for your walls, then consider lighter colors for your floor and ceiling so they act as reflectors. That way your room will still seem bright.

The bathroom vanity is another area where designers often differ in opinion. Some believe that the best way to light a vanity is by placing

**LEFT** This elegant bathroom helps you put your best foot forward with good natural lighting and recessed fixtures on a dimmer. (Photographer: Patty Minnick; room courtesy of Charter Homes and Neighborhoods, Lancaster, Penn.)

**ABOVE** Light, open, and bright—this little bathroom is perfectly starfish simple. And the lighting is placed so that it is in front of you as you look in the mirror, creating more light by reflection. (Photographer: Lynn Noble; Interior Designer: Gail Dunn)

the fixtures on either side of the mirror. Others believe that the best light source should come from above the mirror. The reality is that very few bathrooms easily accommodate the side-lit format, so most vanities are lit from above. If you can accommodate side lighting in your bathroom, choose a fixture with 100 watts for both sides of the mirror. In a perfect world, I would use three sources: a lamp on both sides and another above.

You can also add accent lighting to a bathroom by hanging a chandelier. It adds elegance and sparkle and instantly makes a bathroom or powder room special. Powder rooms are a great place to create drama. Because you spend so little time in them, take your decorating style to the maximum level by being bolder. Accent something important, whether it's a painting, a sculpture, or simply a wall. Have fun with this space.

# NOW DO IT YOURSELF

- **Consider all the activities throughout the day that take place in your spaces.** Now think about the best type of light to make these activities easier, more pleasant, or more efficient. Remember that all rooms should have layers of light that specifically address the different tasks or activities taking place within them.

- **Are there particular items that you treasure and would like to have highlighted?** Investigate the options that would be most attractive. When attempting to light a glass object, it is best to use a twofold approach: Light it from the bottom and the top. When lighting artwork, be careful not to create a reflection of your light fixture in the glass that covers the artwork.

- **In more complex situations, consider investing in a design consultation with a lighting expert; this can result in a better designed system and save you money in the long run.**

# CHAPTER 6

# Up, Down, and All Around

- STEP 1: WALLS AND CEILINGS
- STEP 2: THE NATURAL PATH
- STEP 3: SOMETHING SOFT BENEATH YOUR FEET
- STEP 4: DECORATING WITH FABRICS
- STEP 5: WONDERFUL WINDOWS
- STEP 6: THE ART OF ARRANGING ACCESSORIES

Now that you have a grasp on composition, let's get into some of the details of ornamentation and decoration. When I first began design school I was amazed that we started out by studying the art of cave drawings. From there we moved through the millennia and the centuries of man and his art. It seemed at the time that cave drawings wouldn't be relevant to my career as a designer, but I was surprised when I found myself writing an article on wallcovering patterns that included a stylized version of some of the most important works of art in caves.

Since then, the history of decoration has continued to fascinate me because it is so relevant to my work. For example, when I detail a wall or ceiling with beautiful molding work, it is helpful to have an understanding of the workmanship of the skilled craftsmen who were responsible for some of the greatest homes in history. Studying design abroad gave me a vast array of resources to pull from. I may be biased because I spent more time in Italy than other places, but I think the Italians are the best designers, whether it's shoes, furniture, or architecture. The skilled artisans of history have inspired and directed me in ways that I might otherwise never have imagined. Whether I'm designing walls, ceilings, floors, or beautifully draped window hangings, it's all in the details when it comes to creating exquisite decoration. So let's explore some of the incredible options available to you today.

# STEP 1: Walls and Ceilings

Ceilings and walls make up the largest volumes of space in a room. As we discussed earlier, one of your walls should be a focal point, but the rest of the wall space should be the complementary backdrop for your furnishings and activities. Of course color plays an important role in how effective the backdrop is in accomplishing the mission of the room. But how you choose to apply color, texture, and pattern is a matter of style and expertise.

## THE WALLPAPER OPTION

For nearly five years, I worked as the spokesperson for the wallpaper industry. I love wallpaper. I fell in love with it at age thirteen when I chose and hung the floral-stripe orchid, pink, white, and gold pattern in my bedroom. It was a girly-girl room and I loved it! Wallpaper has come a long way since then. Today's papers actually peel off the wall without leaving a trace. It's the result of new substrates (the product the pattern is printed on) that are nonwoven and incredibly durable—meaning they go up easily and come down without any duress.

I don't think anything pulls a room together as easily as wallpaper. Whether you choose to place it only on one focal wall or four walls, or go for the dramatic by papering the walls and ceilings, it can look amazing, particularly in a small room. Just remember, if you are papering a ceiling, it's best to use a nondirectional pattern (no up or down) to keep everything in the right perspective. Simple, sweet patterns, such as small florals or tiny checks, can create instant charm, while contemporary prints take you boldly into new directions. The best thing about wallpaper is its limitless patterns and colors. You can choose a trompe l'oeil lattice pattern to transform your kitchen into an indoor garden, or expand the room visually with a large-scale open pattern or a mural. Wallpaper is also the easiest way to give your walls a faux finish.

Recently, I used rich fawn brown, faux finish wallpaper for a client's kitchen. The color made the light-stained cabinets pop, and the pattern added texture and just enough detail to make the room interesting without closing it in. In the dining room, I chose a paper with a deep cocoa brown background and a pattern of multicolored floral bouquets. This was the perfect choice because it is a large dining room with an abundance of natural light. The darker color made the room more intimate—cozier for dining. And the flourish of color from the blooms

**ABOVE** The color and pattern of the wallpaper transforms this dining room into a spectacular oasis. (Photographer: Patty Minnick; room courtesy of Charter Homes and Neighborhoods, Lancaster, Penn.)

gave the room the punch of life that it needed. Complementary green silk draperies finished the room with a timeless touch.

There was a time when almost everyone was willing to tackle wallpaper. Not so true today. So if you are not up to hanging it yourself, then hire the best paperhanger you can find, because proper installation is critical, especially if you have chosen an expensive paper—you do not want to waste it by miscalculating the amount to cut. As technology has improved, so has the quality of paper and our ability to be creative. Many patterns are perfectly suited to today's open floor plans with larger-scale and drop repeat patterns. In a drop repeat pattern, the design is staggered so that only every other strip is identical horizontally, where the repeat falls. It takes two strips of wallcovering to complete the pattern horizontally. A drop repeat allows for a more open feeling pattern—perfect for today's interiors. But it's a bit more difficult to measure and hang.

Hanging paper takes patience and finesse. My paperhanger is the best because he loves to hang paper. If at all possible, hire someone who is a member of the National Guild of Professional Paperhangers. If not, then get recommendations and check out a few installations before signing on the dotted line. The cost will vary and is most often priced per roll: I've found an average price of $32 per roll, but prices may vary in different regions of the country. Whoever is hanging the paper should also do the measuring, so they are responsible if there is not enough. This is important, because you may not be able to get another roll in the same dye lot. Color changes from dye lot to dye lot. Sometimes it's a close match, and sometimes it is not.

## THERE'S ALWAYS PAINT

Paint is still the most widely used form of decoration for walls and ceilings. And here, too, technology has made a difference. Latex paints come in a variety of finishes that make it possible to choose your level of durability based on the room. There are dirt fighters that make it easy to wipe clean. There are paints specifically designed for children's rooms, which resist peeling, blistering, and mildew—and, of course, have an incredibly durable finish. There are also paints that resist moisture for use in kitchens and baths, high-traffic-area paints, ceiling paints, and one-coat-coverage paints. I have found that with better quality paint, I need less than I would with a less expensive paint.

Creative painting techniques have been around for centuries. Textures, patterns, broken color techniques (involving multiple colors), glazes and washes, and even Venetian style plaster

techniques have become easier to accomplish with today's technology. Unique finishes can turn a room into a luxurious work of art. One of my recent projects involved a four-step faux paint process, combined with stenciling, to transform a spacious grand room into a warm and inviting gathering space. The rich russet color highlighted with subtle gold stenciling, in a 40-inch repeat pattern, brought the room into proportion while adding just the right amount of depth and quality. With 28-foot ceilings, wallpaper simply could not do the job; a roll of paper is just not long enough for a room with such a high ceiling. With paint, you are only limited by your imagination, patience, and willingness to work.

Another idea that has been around for centuries started with a simple garden trellis. By adopting this basic idea you can create an embellishment with distinction. Whether you choose to hang an outdoor trellis indoors as artwork against a colorful wall or create an entire room of trelliswork, it's a beautiful way to adorn and transform a space. This open framework can be loose and flowing or a proliferation of decorative details; usually real or artificial plants are not part of the design, but of course you could include them if you wish. Treillage and latticework give a room architectural character that cannot be accomplished any other way. It's the perfect way to bring the outdoors in, with light patterns and shadows that look fabulous night and day. I love when the symmetry of a regular patterned trellis is combined with

**LEFT** This charmingly purple bedroom feels fresh and sophisticated while demonstrating the power of paint in creating the perfect backdrop for the bright and cheery drapery fabric. (Photographer: Patty Minnick; room courtesy of Charter Homes and Neighborhoods, Lancaster, Penn.)

whimsy and refreshing detail such as circles and floral sprays. But you don't have to be a carpenter, because you can "paint" yourself a garden trellis room if you have the patience and determination. To do this, first draw the trellis patterns on the wall and then paint them; lots of measuring and fine handwork is required so this project is only for perfectionists! Whether you go with paint or actual latticework, you're the one who decides how much detail to include, selects the colors, and plans where to put the design, which works just as well on ceilings as it does on walls. I suggest, whatever method you choose, that you start with graph paper and lay out the details inch by inch.

## A CARPENTER'S TOUCH

Moving further into the realm of carpentry, let's examine ideas for moldings, wainscoting, and paneling. There was a time when these required the precision of an engineer and the craftsmanship of a fine finish carpenter. Today, most manufacturers do the hard part for you. You send them your measurements and they make the materials fit the job. Of course, the more details you want, the more difficult the installation process. A lot can be achieved with minimal carpentry skills, but there are plenty of well-skilled professionals for hire who can help make your dream room come true.

Covering the most vulnerable portions of a wall—those areas that come into constant contact with hands, feet, elbows, and other agents of abuse—with wood paneling or wainscoting provides an attractive and decorative wall treatment that is tough enough to withstand daily living. Paneling covers the entire wall; it can be simple board against board or it can be highly stylized with deeply carved panels. Wainscoting

goes only partially up the wall, starting at the floor; it usually ends with a chair rail and has drywall above. Wainscoting or paneling transforms a bland space into an elegant room by adding interesting detail that ordinary drywall just doesn't have. Today's production techniques make installation a viable option for many homeowners. You can choose from flat, raised, beaded, and appliquéd panel styles. You simply choose a style and send your measurements to the manufacturer, who matches your dimensions with stock sizes. Wainscot kits include baseboard, rails, stiles (vertical moldings), as well as a top cap, either 36 or 42 inches high. What makes this molding combination unique is that you can adjust the position of the vertical stiles at any point along the horizontal rail. That means the paneled sections can be

proportioned to suit each wall's dimensions, giving a high-quality custom-built look. A typical installation takes only one day and is easy to paint. I have demonstrated how easy it is to install such a kit for Scripps Networks' Ask DIY television show. Similar systems are available for complete wall paneling.

One of my favorite ways to tame an open floor plan is by highlighting a wall. One client had a very tall wall in her foyer that ran from the front door through the living room and into the kitchen. To create a sense of proportion and definition, I used fluted moldings horizontally at the 9-foot height. I added vertical fluted moldings 40 inches apart, creating three different framed areas. In the center framed area, I placed a mirror that filled the entire opening. Then I painted the two framed sections on the sides in a deep terra cotta color. This created a fabulous decorative effect while accomplishing the goals of defining the space and controlling the height.

## THE FIFTH WALL

Don't put your nail gun down just yet, because we are about to hit the ceiling. Yes, ceiling panel systems, tile, and molding are all great options when it comes to adding character and style to a room. Do you remember as a child lying on your bed and staring at the ceiling?

That's a good exercise when it comes to decorating because it will give you a new perspective. As the fifth wall of your room, ceilings are important and should be styled to match the rest of your room. Ceiling tiles, such as the old tin Victorian style, or panels with geometric texture add a historic flair with their beautiful three-dimensionality. The lower your ceiling, the more impact such an installation will have. And they can be painted any color you like, including metallic shades. A simple way to add luxury and sophistication to your home is to combine different textures and materials in your rugs, fabrics, and ceiling.

Decorative tongue-and-groove ceiling planks and panels add warmth and contrast with the natural texture of wood. The richness of wood

adds warmth to any room. I love a ceiling panel system on vaulted ceilings. It's a way of adding interest without creating conflict for the rest of your finishes and surfaces. A warm-toned stain complemented by white moldings or beams can make a cold space feel rich. These systems attach directly to the existing ceiling with virtually no loss in ceiling height. They are generally available in tongue-and-groove designs in 6 by 48 inches, 5 by 78 inches, or 5 by 84 inches.

**OPPOSITE** Tin Look ceiling tiles replicate pressed metal ceilings of the past; these are in the Wellington pattern and add a subtle decorative element to this charming foyer. Though the tiles can be painted, this homeowner chose to leave them in their original state for an understated accent to the Georgian style. (Photo courtesy of Armstrong Ceilings)

**RIGHT** The WoodHaven ceiling planks in Rustic Pine draw attention to the dramatic cathedral ceilings, while adding a cozy, warm element to this eating area. (Photo courtesy of Armstrong Ceilings)

## DON'T FORGET THE TRIM

But there is more for your ceilings and walls than just paneling. Moldings have made a comeback. For too many years, new homes lacked character because there was no attention to detail in moldings. You were lucky if your home had baseboards. The good news is that this is another area where new technology has made the production of moldings less expensive and more readily available. Originally, moldings were made of plaster. Today they are made of wood, MDF (medium density fiberboard), and hard polystyrene foam. The result is incredible detail at an affordable price. Cornice and crown moldings add style, opulence, and exceptional visual appeal to an otherwise unadorned space. Just think about what makes so many of the historic, older homes so interesting. It's all in the details at the ceiling, on the walls, and at archways and doorways.

Cornice moldings, layers of moldings, ceiling medallions, and coffered ceilings (ceilings with recessed square panels, bordered with trim for ornamental purposes) are now seen in most new homes to some degree or another. In fact, we almost expect it. And we should.

**BELOW**  The opulent, visually appealing coffered ceiling in this master bedroom provides an interesting place for the eye to rest while you relax on the bed. (Photographer: Patty Minnick; room courtesy of Charter Homes and Neighborhoods, Lancaster, Penn.)

**OPPOSITE (TOP)**  The faux painted sky on this towering ceiling gives the space an unending view; the angled molding at the corners gives the illusion of a vaulted ceiling, when in reality it is flat. (Photographer: Lynn Noble; Interior Designer: Gail Dunn)

**OPPOSITE (BOTTOM)**  Open rafters give this room the details and coziness that are necessary in a truly Cottage style space. (Photographer: Lori Stahl; Interior Designer: Sharon Hanby-Robie)

But don't be dismayed if your home is missing these finishing details because it's not that difficult to add them. My own home had virtually no molding detail. Over the years, I have added a little here and a little there. Because I am not up to fighting with a miter box (which lets you cut molding to fit into corners), I hire my local carpenter friend to take care of such details.

Like so many other aspects of your home, the goal should be a cohesive plan that can be implemented over time. If you choose to add crown molding, take into consideration all the rooms where you would like to add such a detail and choose a molding that can be adapted to all those rooms. When you are finished, it will look

like original work rather than something that was added on in stages.

You can also add columns, arches, and even niches and ceiling domes if you like. One of my favorite details is to create an accent wall. There are endless ways to mix and match different trims with varying wainscot systems to create a custom-looking accent wall. To make a room look luxurious without calling a carpenter, you can combine stiles (vertical moldings) with horizontal moldings to create a series of squares, and then finish them off with crown molding at the top and large-scale baseboard at the bottom. There are do-it-yourself kits that fit together easily for a professional custom look that most homeowners can achieve themselves in a matter of hours.

## NOW DO IT YOURSELF

- **Consider your walls a backdrop for everything that happens.** They should be an integral component of the composition. They should complement or enhance the total environment with color, texture, and pattern.

- **Spend a little time staring up at your ceiling and dream about how you can give it dimension and focus.**

# STEP 2: The Natural Path

The good news is that there are more choices than ever before when it comes to flooring. The bad news is that there are so many options that it's hard to choose! For example, not so long ago choosing a wood floor was simply a matter of selecting a wood and a stain color. Your basic choices were pine and oak available in several different stain colors, and perhaps the choice of shiny or matte finish.

Dark floors are all the rage. Some say they make a room look larger, though I am not sure on this one. They are definitely dramatic and are perfect for making light furniture stand out. Dark stains include tints barely distinguishable from black, chocolate colors, and deep reddish tones—this variety makes them much more interesting than simply black. I consider this depth of color more on the formal side, making

it desirable for Contemporary or Traditional style furnishings with an elegant flair.

**OPPOSITE (TOP)**   The complementary textures, particularly the rough-hewn ceiling beams, give this room its distinctively Southwest character. (Photographer: MontesBurksCreative— Santa Fe; room courtesy of Deborah Durham)

**OPPOSITE (BOTTOM)**   A few simple moldings strategically placed create the fabulous focal wall behind the bed. (Illustrator: Patty Minnick)

**BELOW**   Wide-planked pine flooring enhances the beauty and style of simple Shaker living. The contrast between the dark floors and the light-colored cabinets creates interest and makes both stand out. (Photographer: Patty Minnick; room courtesy of Steven L. Edris, Builder, Lancaster, Penn.)

If your preference is something a bit lighter, there are lots of crisp, clean, and elegant floor tones to choose from. Natural blond woods such as ash, maple, or white oak and pine can create a calming spirit in a room. Pickled floors that are nearly white with a semi-opaque whitewash are softer and less formal. Bleached or scrubbed woods such as pine or oak are the perfect complement for Contemporary spaces or even Swedish country style rooms.

## CHOOSE FROM WOODS

But it's not just the color of floors that makes them fresh and new. Today, hardwood flooring is more beautiful and durable than ever with options such as red oak, pine, Brazilian cherry, bird's-eye maple, Australian cypress, and bamboo. And although you can still find some bare boards to install and stain, most of today's wood floors are prefinished. The advantage is that the finishing process is done in a controlled setting and the products used are so durable that many come with ten-year warranties. Some woods have even been impregnated with resins to make them nearly indestructible. Of course, with all these choices also comes a range of prices. The key to a wood's durability and appearance is a combination of the wood

**BELOW**  The city beyond the windows is the focal point, but a classic wood floor sets a sophisticated stage for the totally contemporary scene within. (Photo courtesy of Armstrong Floors)

**OPPOSITE**  The richly hewn floor provides a strong and harmonious foundation for the heavy carved furnishings, architectural details, and highly textured art and accessories. (Photo courtesy of Armstrong Floors)

species, the grade, the cut, and the finish. The fewer flaws a piece of wood has and the more consistent its color, the better its quality.

Bamboo flooring, like wood, can also be found in a variety of styles and qualities. Similar in appearance to wood, bamboo has recently grown in popularity because it is considered a "green," or environmentally sound, material. One big difference between bamboo and wood is that less of the material goes to waste: The entire bamboo stalk (which can grow to 125 feet tall) can be used for flooring, while only the basic trunk of the tree can be used for floor

boards. And, unlike trees, bamboo does not need to be replanted to be regenerated; it is highly prolific and will regrow on its own. Often natural bamboo is bleached to make the color lighter. If you prefer a darker color, consider carbonized bamboo, which is sent through a heating process that darkens it (but also makes it slightly less hard). Bamboo floors are made by taking the long, individual strips of the grass and gluing them together. Look for strips that are ⅝ inch thick for good quality. You can find thinner bamboo, but I don't recommend it. The strips are generally produced in 3½- or 6-inch widths. Bamboo is hard wearing and water resistant, making it an interesting alternative to standard wood floors. It has a fresh, sleek, modern feel when installed because its lines are cleaner than pine or oak.

The biggest news in wood flooring is patterning. Parquet flooring has come a long way since its last heyday of square patterns. Inventive new formats that mix traditional patterns with modern ideas make appearances all over the house in the form of medallions, interlocking spheres, diagonally intersected squares, and even cobbleblock designs made of round slices of wood logs. Foyers, living and dining rooms,

even kitchens and bedrooms are benefiting from new patterns that create subtle or astonishing effects with center inlays or simple geometric borders.

The good news is these inlays are much more affordable than they used to be, so you can create a luxurious feeling without spending a ton of money. What accounts for the new affordability of inlays and medallions is today's technology (specifically laser cutting), which makes it much easier to create them. In the old days, they all had to be handcarved. A medallion should be about one-third of the width of the room. For example, if your room is 20 feet long by 15 feet wide, your medallion can be 5 feet (60 inches) in diameter. Pricing will vary, but for a medallion that incorporates five different woods in a very intricate pattern, expect to pay about $1,550 for one that is 48 inches in diameter.

Beyond center medallions another idea that I like is overall parquet patterns with lots of details—nothing like the old style parquet you may remember. A fancy pattern that incorporates four different wood species can cost about $30 per square foot plus installation. Parquet can be glued down to a plywood subfloor or concrete. Wood borders are available in a variety of interesting and creative patterns and can be used to define a specific area or to upscale a room by surrounding it with detail.

Wood borders are also a great way to unify or blend two opposing wood floors in adjoining rooms. For example, many of us are changing out our old kitchen tile or resilient flooring for wood floors. Often an adjoining dining room or living room already has a wood floor that cannot be matched. By simply using a multi-wood pattern border you can easily make

**OPPOSITE**  The softly stained floor adds contrast in color and texture, contributing to the overall airy feel of this room. (Photo courtesy of Armstrong Floors)

**RIGHT**  Art meets the floor when you include an inlaid medallion. This sketch illustrates the beauty and detail that an inlay can add to a room. (Illustrator: Patty Minnick)

the transition from one wood floor to another. Preassembled border modules can be glued down just like parquet flooring. Just remember that if you want to add an inlay to your hardwood floor, decide on it before you lay the first plank. Plan your floor design and have an expert in wood floor installation take a look at it; you want to be sure that your floor and border are the same height when installed. You also want to carefully plan your furniture arrangement so you don't end up with the floor details in the wrong place.

## A NEW LOOK IN LEATHER

One newer designer trend that has a centuries-old history is leather. Real leather is seductive and inviting to touch. Leather floor tiles are sturdy, versatile, and incredibly fashionable. Leather tile is generally ⅛ inch thick and can take daily nicks, scratches, and even spills and incorporate them into a rich, mellow patina. Leather tiles are available in a variety of patterns, both smooth and textured, and in an array of natural or dyed colors. What I love most about leather flooring is its ability to reflect any style from sophisticated to sassy to rugged or sumptuous. Best of all it's a natural sound absorber, which makes it perfect for noisy spaces. I avoid using leather with a sprayed-on pigment and a polyurethane film coating, because ultimately the coating will wear off and so too will the sprayed-on pig-

ment. My preference is to use aniline-finished leather—full-grain leather that has been soaked in aniline, a penetrating dye, and does not have any other coating. This treatment results in soft, pliable leather, with the natural grain showing through.

Best of all, leather allows for a lot of creativity. It can be embossed to resemble a variety of exotic hides such as lizard, alligator, buffalo, elephant, or hippo. And the design possibilities are endless. Laser-etched borders, etched area rug designs (within a wall-to-wall leather floor), and etched corner scrolls are just a few of the options available in leather. For more leather flooring ideas, visit www.interiorsurfaces.com.

## DURABLE TILES AND STONES

When it comes to tile, the possibilities are bigger than ever and I'm not just talking about size—although generous 24- and 48-inch tiles of natural stone are available. But what makes this category of flooring so exciting is the incredible variety of choices, from natural stone to ceramic to glass to metal. I still prefer natural stone to almost any other medium and recently specified granite tiles for a client's kitchen floor. For the adjoining family room floor I used bird's-eye maple hardwood that matches the kitchen cabinets. The dark, rich, varied-color granite is the perfect contrast for the light tones of the bird's-eye maple. I repeated the granite on the countertop of the island to give the space a cohesive look that wasn't distracting.

Natural stone floors offer a distinct and beautiful flooring choice. Slate, marble, travertine, limestone, and granite are all considered natural stones, and each has its own unique appearance and appeal. Slate, with its dramatic multicolored blends, is perfect for Tudor or Craftsman decorating styles. It also nicely complements a rustic Contemporary style. Marble floors have been used for centuries, and add an aura of sophistication to a room. Marble can be found in a multitude of colors and style, including emerald green, dark imperial green, black, cream, pink, brown, white, and more. All sizes and thicknesses are available. Marble should be polished to give it a patina that not only enhances its beauty, but also makes it easier to live with by helping to keep stains out. I recommend cleaning products designed specifically

**OPPOSITE** This Tuscan style dining room radiates comfort and strength with its rich textures, from the stone of the large tiles and the table base to the complex weave and pattern of the chair fabric. (Photographer: MontesBurksCreative—Santa Fe)

**ABOVE** Dramatic and visually appealing from all views, the inlaid border in this foyer floor creates classic impact and acts as the perfect frame for an octagonal rug. (Photographer: Patty Minnick; Interior Designer: Sharon Hanby-Robie)

for polished stone floors to extend the life of the finish.

Limestone is more casual than marble. Its style is upscale but comfortable. I consider granite upscale and I think it is perfect for Transitional styles. In choosing any cut natural stone, it's important to make sure it is recommended for floors. Some are not strong enough and should only be used for walls. I always recommend working with a licensed professional stone mason when purchasing or installing natural stone products in order to guarantee the best results. Look at large samples, such as full-size tiles, and ask about the potential variation.

Remember that with natural stone, as with any natural product, you can expect imperfections. These imperfections only add to the aesthetic appeal and won't devalue your new floor. If imperfections are something that you cannot live with, choose ceramic tile instead. Ceramic and porcelain tiles provide some of the most versatile design possibilities with an endless array of colors, textures, and designs. Ceramic tiles are made from clay or a mixture of organic materials; ceramic tile is finished by kiln firing. Tile is made in many shapes and sizes, and it is glazed or unglazed. It can be found in tiny tiles for mosaic applications or in large, sheet-like squares of ceramic. Porcelain tiles are becoming more available than in the past, and therefore, more affordable. They look like stone but do not have to be sealed to avoid staining or odor absorption, so they are easy to maintain.

Of course, an endless selection of clay and ceramic tile is available. The big news here is size and variety of installation. I usually mix three to four different sizes or shapes to create a sophisticated but relaxed scheme that works well with the way most of us live today. When I first started specifying this mixed-size pattern style, the installers balked. But they have become accustomed to this design and recognize that it's a much more interesting look than simply laying tiles square.

One of my favorite newer types is glass tiles. They are available in clear or frosted finishes. But here, too, the styles seem to be endless. The overall effect of glass tile is that it glows. It's ethereal. I love the way light plays off it and makes it shimmer. It is available for both floors and walls. Many decorative glass accents are available that are perfect as insets or borders within or around ceramic tile.

Choosing a floor is a very important step in your decorating. It's also one of the most expensive and lasting features, so choose well. Just as I have suggested throughout this book,

the key is to establish your own style, then orchestrate it uniquely in your own way. Know yourself. Be realistic about how often you will change something as important as a floor.

If your intention is to change your flooring every ten years, then I encourage you to be less conservative and enjoy adding a little more detail and interest to your home. But if you are not inclined to make changes, stick with something that is classic in style—you can never go wrong with a classic design. If you are unsure, then ask for help. It's well worth getting a professional involved. Also keep in mind whether you will be adding a rug to your hardwood or tile floor. This too can affect your decision. For example, for one of my clients, we purposely chose to create an inlaid border into the mahogany wood floor in her foyer because we knew that we would be placing an octagon-shaped rug there as well. The two were meant to be together; it was how we planned it.

## NOW DO IT YOURSELF

■ **Always draw out a floor plan when making a decision for a floor with any pattern.** Many retailers have computer-aided programs that can show you the overall effect of your design choice. If you are working on a whole-house floor plan, it's critical that you lay it out and plan for transitions from one surface to another. I have found that wood always moves. It shrinks in colder temperatures and swells in warm, humid climates. If you are planning on it butting up to tile, recognize that it will pull away and create a small crack-like space between the grout and the wood. This is normal.

# STEP 3: Something Soft beneath Your Feet

Hard-surface flooring is all the rage and I expect that it will continue to be popular for years to come, because flooring such as tile, stone, wood, and laminate are incredibly durable and therefore long lasting. But a soft comfy rug feels so good underfoot. As I've said before, I love area rugs in particular, because they offer so many different styles. Change the style of your rug and you change the feel of your room instantly. Every room needs a good foundation for style, and an area rug is one of the simplest ways to give your room direction, color, and a signature all its own. I don't know exactly how many different area rugs are available, but www.csnrugs.com has more than ten thousand styles available. With that many options, it can certainly be confusing. Let me start by categorizing a few of the more popular styles.

## ORIENTAL RUGS

Today a rug's descriptive name indicates where the design originated and not necessarily where the rug was made. The term "oriental" used to define rugs that came from the East, the vast region the European explorers traveled to as they crossed over the Mediterranean Sea and

**BELOW** The strong pattern and color of this Williamsburg style rug is the foundation for a most inviting family room. (Photographer: Lori Stahl; Interior Designer: Sharon Hanby-Robie)

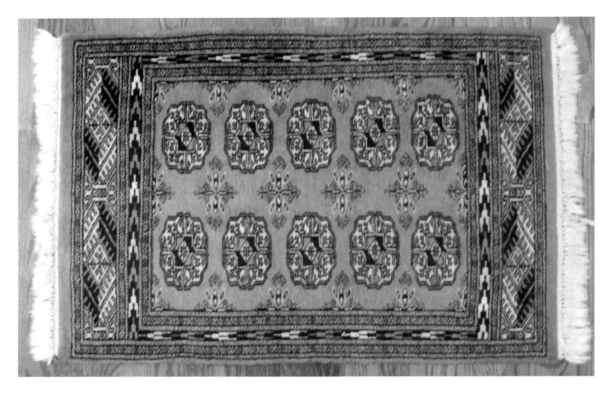

circled the most southern tip of Africa. Today *oriental* refers to a large category of rugs inspired by any one of the original styles characteristic of those regions. The original oriental rugs were made for utilitarian purposes such as blankets and floor mats, which made a comfortable place to sleep. Traveling tribes of shepherds made these rugs for their own use. Eventually, rug weaving evolved into an art of handcrafted rugs that included a variety of weaves from flat-weave (no pile) to cushiony, hand-knotted pile, and a variety of other techniques, each with its own unique design.

Oriental rugs feature intricate patterns with specific features associated with specific tribes of weavers. The ancient rugs could easily be identified by the motifs and patterns that the tribe incorporated. The original rugs were completely

made by hand. Wool was sheared from sheep and goats and spun into yarns that were woven on looms. You can still find many hand-knotted rugs; in fact, I think there are more available today than ever, resulting in more affordable choices. But there is also an enormous selection of machine-made rugs that are of very good quality and even more affordable. In fact, some think that today's technology makes it possible to create more intricate and detailed patterns than you can find in the handmade rugs.

Oriental rugs fall into two broad design categories: Turkish and Persian. Turkish designs are based on tribal patterns of nomadic weavers and tend to be geometric, angular, and more primitive looking, while the Persian designs are based on rugs made in controlled urban settings. They tend to be curvilinear, floral, and finely detailed.

I love oriental style rugs because they work with virtually any style of decoration. And they are still some of the most long-lasting rugs made. Most of them will outlive us. I use them everywhere and never hesitate to use them at entryways. They are durable and the pattern camouflages most dirt. To clean, simply roll them up and take them to a professional cleaner. For large-scale rugs, have the professional come to your home to clean the rugs.

One of my favorites is Bokhara style rugs, with their simple geometric design that works well in any space and easily complements other oriental style carpets. The design is dominated by rows of guls (symbolic shapes) and surrounding geometric patterns. One legend says that one particular symbol of guls represented elephant footprints, and still other gul patterns represented birds and other animals. Today Bokhara style rugs are made across the carpet-weaving world, including Pakistan, Iran, India, Turkey, Afghanistan, and Central Asia.

Other examples of oriental and Persian style rugs are kilims and dhurries. These flat-weave rugs with less refined weaves and patterns were originally made by nomadic tribes and used as blankets. Native American and Central American tribal rugs have similar characteristics. Less formal in style, these tribal rugs are

**OPPOSITE** Bokhara rugs can be incorporated into almost any setting. Their strong geometrical pattern mixes well with other oriental style carpets. I use them often in foyers and hallways because they can handle the traffic. (Photographer: Patty Minnick)

**RIGHT** I believe that a rug can be the heart and soul of a room. This tribal Persian reproduction adds an unusual and unique element in this family's kitchen. (Photographer: Patty Minnick; Interior Designer, Sharon Hanby-Robie)

perfect for casual spaces both Traditional and Contemporary. I also like a flat-weave rug for kitchens—just be careful because some flat-weave rugs curl up at the edges, which can cause you to trip.

One of the key elements to any rug is its color. And this is particularly true when choosing a simpler flat-weave style, which may have large sections of nearly solid color. The visible difference between a high-quality chemically dyed rug and a naturally dyed rug is often subtle. However, less expensive chemically dyed rugs are often dyed with aniline-based dyes, which are not as stable and can damage wool

fiber yarns. An easy way to check the quality of the dye is to rub a section of the rug with a damp cloth to see if the dye comes off.

## AUBUSSON AND SAVONNERIE RUGS

For more formal decorating, I like the look of Aubusson and Savonnerie rugs. These rugs, which originated in France around the fifteenth century, are perfect for Traditional style furniture. These elegant, floral rugs usually feature a center medallion surrounded by an open field. Originally Aubussons were flat-weaves. But today you can find many that have been adapted for modern living with a lush, thick pile. Savonnerie rugs have always been pile carpets. They look similar to Persians but with a more impressionistic quality that is highly appealing, almost romantic.

## TRANSITIONAL, CONVERSATIONAL, AND CONTEMPORARY RUGS

As the popularity of area rugs has increased, so too has the variety of new styles. I call these Transitional rugs because they often combine Contemporary and Traditional elements in one rug. They can be Classic or Modern, depending on how you decorate around them. Their versatility makes them an easy choice. One of the strongest styles is floral. Floral, garden, and botanical styles have a sophisticated design that is inviting and naturally harmonious in color and design. They make a room feel fresh. I used a floral rug in my master bathroom—it absolutely makes the space. Another floral style that is popular and more romantic is the less formal style known as European Country or shabby style. It has a more subtle but yet inviting air that easily enhances any room. Soft pastel colors dominate this style, making it perfect

for bedrooms. In general, floral rugs add color and make a room feel easy and breezy.

Another category of area rugs that has found its place in our homes, particularly kitchens, is what I call "conversational" rugs. These fun rugs embrace the fun of food as decoration. Eggplants, carrots, radishes, peppers, and even asparagus become the center of attention on these friendly rugs. Many of them are made of cotton, which is soft underfoot. They are available in wool and acrylic as well. Sometimes fruits and flowers join hands for a very merry bit of floor excitement in a conversational rug. Or you may find the little pig that went to market daringly posing in the center of a wonderful round rug. Other conversational inspirations come from nautical themes, football, baseball, beach, and even mountains. These rugs are meant to add a little fun to your décor.

Contemporary rugs have developed into an exquisite array of styles with a vast range of patterns and materials that are spectacular. Circles, squares, swirls, and abstract patterns can give your room a bold brush of color and style. If you love Contemporary or Urban décor, these rugs are perfect for you. Even if your furniture is a bit more Traditional, these rugs can give your rooms a fresh Transitional feel. For added texture, choose a rug in which the pattern is highlighted by embossing or carving. An embossed rug is produced with a high-low weaving technique that creates the illusion of embossing. In a carved rug the pile is literally carved with a blade to create a detailed highlight around some of the individual features in the pattern, such as the flowers.

## ANIMAL SKINS

Animal skins have been used as floor cloths for centuries. Today authentic cowhides are making statements with their handsome style. Whether it's a lodge style or simply a rustic bedroom that you're dreaming about, a cowhide rug makes a nice addition. If you are thinking about something a bit more exotic, then you might like to consider a zebra, Bengal tiger,

**OPPOSITE** The floral sprays of this garden-inspired rug add softness and comfort to this Cottage style bedroom. (Photographer: Lori Stahl; Interior Designer: Sharon Hanby-Robie)

**BELOW** The bold colors and block patterns of this Contemporary rug add pizzazz to this family room. (Photographer: Patty Minnick; room courtesy of Charter Homes and Neighborhoods, Lancaster, Penn.)

giraffe, or even a leopard stenciled cowhide. If the idea of a cowhide doesn't match your style but you like animal prints, you can choose from many fun animal print area rugs made of wool, nylon, and acrylic. They are bold with contrasting color but work beautifully with many furniture styles to create an exotic and adventurous decorating style. They are perfect with leather-upholstered furnishings.

## FIBER RUGS

One of my favorite fibers for rugs is sisal. This natural fiber is durable and fun and ever more popular. I started using sisal rugs both as area and wall-to-wall rugs almost twenty years ago. Sisal can be dyed to any color and can be easily hand painted for a truly custom look. And it's very affordable. A 9 by 12-foot rug with a fabric banded border costs less than $500.

If you are looking for an incredibly durable and easy-to-care-for rug, consider using an outdoor rug indoors. This is a growing market, so the variety of colors, styles, and textures will continue to expand. These rugs look like cotton but are made of polypropylene or DuraCord (the same material that hammocks are made of). These are water, mildew, and stain resistant. And best of all, they can be hosed down for cleaning.

**BELOW** The strategic placement of flat-weave primitive rugs defines and highlights the best of this Shaker-inspired hearth room. (Photographer: Patty Minnick; room courtesy of Steven L. Edris, Builder, Lancaster, Penn.)

**OPPOSITE** This sunroom makes the transition from outdoors to indoors with light and natural materials such as the sisal rug. (Photographer: Patty Minnick; room courtesy of Charter Homes and Neighborhoods, Lancaster, Penn.)

Ultimately, the variety of rugs available makes it easy to find a place to begin your decorating scheme or a wonderful way of pulling it all together. Whether you love patterns or are just looking for something that feels good to your bare toes, a rug that makes you smile is a great addition to any room.

## NOW DO IT YOURSELF

■ **Always, always use a rug pad under all your rugs.** Not only does it help keep them in place, but more importantly, it helps keep rugs from being stretched out of shape. In addition, it makes thinner or less expensive rugs last longer and feel better. You can easily find inexpensive rug pads, but I prefer something with a bit more to offer. My favorites include WunderFirm and Vantage Industries' Tenacious Hold rug pads. What makes these pads unique is that they have a dense, firm rubber waffle base on one side to secure the rug to the floor, with a scruffy fabric on the other side that holds your rug while protecting it from heel punctures and heavy traffic stress. It is thick enough to hide irregularities in stone and tile surfaces so your rug looks smooth. It can also be reversed if you want to place your area rug on a wall-to-wall rug.

■ **If you have an open floor plan home, area rugs can help delineate one space from another.** By simply placing a rug under or in front of furniture, it makes the setting special. It says, "Look at me." A rug can help organize spaces simply by defining them.

■ **If at all possible, start your decorating scheme by choosing your rug before your other fabrics**

**and colors.** It's so much easier to match those items to a rug than the other way around.

■ **In a bedroom, a rug doesn't need to cover the entire room.** I usually place an area rug half under the bed and allow the rest of it to show.

# STEP 4: Decorating with Fabrics

Fabrics make a room. The personality of your fabric choices will ultimately determine how your room looks and feels. Just consider the differences between a soft, sumptuous, silk embroidered fabric with layers of beautiful threads in an exquisite floral pattern and a thick, rich, natural

leather with an intoxicating aroma. These two fibers create two very distinct atmospheres. Both are luxurious, but in unique ways—one more feminine and the other more masculine.

Fabrics are first divided into two content categories: natural fibers and man-made fibers. Natural fibers are subdivided into *plant* fibers such as cotton and linen, *protein* fibers such as wool and silk, and *mineral* fibers such as glass and asbestos. Natural fibers are very appealing because of their beautiful appearance and also for their distinctive hand (the way they feel and hang). If you are concerned about the environment, then choose natural fibers because they can easily be disposed of safely.

Man-made fabrics can be made from organic products such as wood pulp or cotton waste, which is used to make rayon, or from chemical sources such as olefin, acrylic, polyester, or nylon. Chemically based fabrics are composed of ethylene, propylene, or other fiber-forming substances. Polypropylene fabric is a fabulous example because it's basically a plastic that has been pushed through a sieve to create fibers that are woven into fabric. It cannot absorb water, and therefore is incredibly stain resistant and durable.

Many of today's fabrics are blends of both natural and man-made fiber, which results in the best of all worlds: durability, colorfastness, and a beautiful hand as well. But content is not the only determining factor in a fabric's ability to stand up to real living. Construction also plays a vital role. Obviously the tighter the weave, the stronger the fabric; the more open the weave, the weaker the fabric. But the thickness of each thread also plays a role. One of the best fabrics for durability and touchability is microfiber polypropylene. Picture the finest fiber you can imagine, then divide it in half—that is a microfiber. Half of the thickness of silk and one hundred times finer than a human hair, a microfiber is the tiniest man-made fiber ever created. Fabrics made of microfiber are wrinkle resistant and easy to care for.

My white sectional sofa is upholstered in microfiber, and the sueded finish feels luxurious and soft. As an added plus, microfiber fabric is naturally water repellent due to its construction process and can be waterproof when specially treated. You can find many different styles of fabric made from microfiber. It can be made into an incredibly soft yarn and woven into a warm, soft throw for your sofa, or made into a plush sueded-finish fabric for upholstery.

## MATCH FABRICS WITH FUNCTION

When choosing fabrics it is important that you make sure the fiber matches the function. Obviously, you wouldn't upholster your family room sofa in a fine embroidered silk fabric. But you might consider it for pillows or draperies. In fact, over the last few years, silk has become one of the most popular fabrics for window treatments. But even as a drapery fabric, silk requires special linings and care in how you style the drapery treatment. There are certain treatments silk fabrics are well suited for and

**OPPOSITE**  No need to fear a white sofa if you make the right choice in your fabric. This microfiber-covered sofa is designed for living. (Photographer: Lynn Noble; Interior Designer: Sharon Hanby-Robie)

**BELOW**  I like mixing blush colors with stronger colors for accents such as pillows and art. The luxury of silk embroidered pillows makes this room indulgently comfortable. (Photographer: Lynn Noble; Interior Designer: Sharon Hanby-Robie)

others they are not. Without a bump cloth liner (a light flannel lining that prevents color fading and provides structure and insulation), silk draperies will look limp and inexpensive. But with the proper liner, they flow like a ball gown. Many natural fibers are hydrophilic, which means they will react to humidity. Whenever I use a natural fiber in draperies, I leave a generous hem so that if the fabric shrinks due to humidity, the draperies can be lengthened.

Upholstery fabrics are often graded for their ability to withstand abrasion. The Wyzenbeek test determines how many rubs a fabric can endure before it begins to show wear. A commercial-grade fabric can usually endure about 30,000 rubs. A residential fabric is considered suitable for heavy-duty use when it can endure 15,000 double rubs. This is just part of how the durability of fabrics is determined and should not be considered the ultimate factor.

Most stores offer stain-repellent finishes on upholstered items. And they do work—to some extent. They make fabric stain resistant, not stain proof. The key is that stain-repellent finishes come with a guarantee that the company can remove most stains from your furniture, and if not, will replace it. But honestly, I don't recommend them for wools, which are naturally stain repellent, or textiles such as polypropylene because it is already stain resistant. In the not too distant future, I believe that most fibers will be manufactured with stain-resistant treatments applied before they are woven into textiles.

## CHOOSE FABRICS THAT MAKE YOU SMILE

Now that you have a basic idea of what types of fabrics are available, let's talk about the fun

of fabrics: colors, textures, and patterns! Many people have a fear of mixing patterns. Just like fear of color, it usually has more to do with being afraid of making a mistake than anything else. So let's make this simple. There was a time when decorating was all about matching. Today, it's all about blending. What's the difference? Freedom! Colors don't have to be perfectly matched, but they should be pleasingly complementary and blend nicely. The simplest way to blend colors is to limit the number of colors being used in a given space and then choose a variety of shades and intensities to create your palette. Choose your specific color carefully and then look for fabrics that contain some of that same shade.

I recommend starting with a color theme and then allowing one pattern to dominate. Remember, your color palette should have three dominant colors: a main, a contrasting, and an accent. Use the accent color in three different places within the room. The complementary fabrics should share at least one color with the dominant print. Many fabric manufacturers are now building their fabric books by color, so it is easier to find different patterns in the same color palette.

When it comes to mixing patterns you have several options. One approach is choosing patterns that are similar in scale (the size of an image within a pattern). For example, combine a small floral pattern with a small check pattern. Patterns may be large and obvious or small. Small patterns will often appear as solids when viewed at a distance. This is a technique that Laura Ashley has made famous. Her coordinating miniature prints are charming and always easy to pull together.

On the other hand, a strong pattern can

**OPPOSITE** This fabulously pink bedroom is the perfect example of how to mix and match color and pattern to create delightful results. (Photographer: Patty Minnick; room courtesy of Charter Homes and Neighborhoods, Lancaster, Penn.)

**ABOVE** Each color, pattern, and texture in this family room, from the Williamsburg patterned rug and wallpaper to the Royal Bee patterned pillow, was chosen to create a layered and historically inspired place of comfort. (Photographer: Lori Stahl; Interior Designer: Sharon Hanby-Robie)

inspire a room. Simply use less dominant patterns to complement it. A large floral print pairs nicely with a large-scale geometric pattern. The balance is created by the contrasts that they offer each other. Be careful not to use too many patterns in the same scale because they will compete with each other for attention.

My favorite style for mixing patterns is to use the rule of three: Choose three patterns with three different scales. You might experiment with a large floral pattern, a medium plaid, and a small overall print. To maintain balance, the main fabric should make up two-thirds of what is used, the second fabric should be one-third of what is used, and the third fabric should be used as accent.

There was a time when experts would tell you not to use two different stripes in the same room. I say if you love stripes, use them! Just vary the scale by using narrow stripes in some areas and wider ones in others. And it is perfectly okay to mix stripes with checks, florals, and plaids. We ended up with sixteen different patterns in one client's large living room, including the three oriental carpets. Trust me, it worked beautifully. Of course, always take into consideration adjoining rooms. It's important to have a common color or pattern theme that connects them in some way.

Some of the most exquisite rooms are those that give patterns room to breathe. One way to

accomplish this is to trim your patterns in solid colors or contrasting patterns to separate them from each other. This is particularly true when using several patterns for pillows that will be placed near each other. You can also use a pattern as a border on draperies. It can be as simple as a 3-inch border added to the interior edge of the drapery panel, or as bold as an 18-inch hem of pattern on a solid drapery panel. But you can also give your patterns breathing room simply by placing them against a solid color. Unfussy backgrounds allow the foreground of pattern to stand out. Similarly, highly textured fabrics benefit from being placed against a nontextured solid.

Speaking of textures—one of my favorites is leather. I love leather because it never gets hot or sticky, or cold or clammy like vinyl. This natural fiber breathes and takes on the room temperature. Also, leather tanning has come a long way. Today's leathers require very little care. Most are dyed all the way through, so even if you do scratch the surface, the color will still be consistent. And most also have a protective finish that makes them even more resistant to scratches than ever before. Of course, you can find some unfinished leathers that are intended to absorb oils and stains to create a magnificent patina. But I don't recommend unfinished leather for families with small children or pets!

**LEFT** Floral, plaid, and mini-print fabric patterns work compatibly in scale and color to give this master bedroom warmth and color. (Photographer: Patty Minnick; room courtesy of Charter Homes and Neighborhoods, Lancaster, Penn.)

**OPPOSITE** It takes so little effort to add a contrasting border to the edges of a drapery treatment, yet the effect is so striking. (Photographer: Patty Minnick; room courtesy of Charter Homes and Neighborhoods, Lancaster, Penn.)

However, a coated leather will take the punishment of real living with nary a mark. And the really good news is that if you are a cat owner, like me, cats are not likely to find leather a good scratching post, so it's the perfect fabric for cats with claws. Leather is available in hundreds of colors and textures. Just wipe clean with a damp cloth when soiled.

tern will appear heavier or larger than if covered in a light pattern. Use bolder prints to make a room appear smaller, and airier mini-prints to enlarge it.

■ **As a rule of thumb to keep from creating chaos, use no more than four different patterns in a room.** But distribute them throughout the space to avoid creating a cluttered or unbalanced appearance.

## NOW DO IT YOURSELF

■ **Make sure all your patterns have the same neutral color as their background.** In other words, don't mix a warm cream background pattern with a pure white or gray background pattern. The white will make the others appear dirty.

■ **Remember to consider the overall effect the pattern will have in a specific application.** For example, a chair covered in a bright or dark pat-

## STEP 5: Wonderful Windows

For me, dressing windows beautifully is akin to shopping for a new outfit. First you have to decide what style is right for the occasion. Then you must figure out what best suits your shape, and, finally, you must choose just the right accessories to complete the ensemble. As

an interior designer, I have seen just about every style of window treatment ranging from layers and layers of silk fabric puddling on the floor to almost no treatment at all. Today's trend is truly about simple, sophisticated, and appropriate.

Window treatments are divided into *hard* and *soft*. Hard window treatments are functional and give you the ability to control light. They include blinds, shutters, and the like. Their vanes or slats can be tilted to control the amount of light entering a room. They usually can be pulled up out of the way for an unobstructed view. Soft treatments cover a larger category of products such as roller shades, cellular shades, pleated shades, roman shades, solar shades, woven shades, and draperies. One of my favorite and most popular shades is Silhouette for windows and Luminette for sliding doors, both from Hunter Douglas. They combine the function of blinds with the softness of sheer draperies. Imagine two panels of sheer fabric, back to back, with fabric slats between that can be tilted to control light. They can be used as

**LEFT (TOP)** From the Royal Bee detail on the silk fabric to the rope cording and the tassel fringe, these draperies are all about style and romance. (Photographer: Lori Stahl; Interior Designer: Sharon Hanby-Robie)

**LEFT (BOTTOM)** Russet-colored cotton damask has the perfect feel and texture for a simple but elegantly crafted box-pleated valance with panels that spill luxuriously onto the floor. (Photographer: Patty Minnick; room courtesy of Charter Homes and Neighborhoods, Lancaster, Penn.)

**OPPOSITE** Charming touches create a dreamy nursery. The drapery panels can easily be removed when the baby becomes mobile, and returned later. (Photographer: Patty Minnick; room courtesy of Charter Homes and Neighborhoods, Lancaster, Penn.)

they are or dressed up with a drapery treatment such as silk side panels.

Many newer homes have entire walls of windows that definitely make a statement all on their own. Often, I will add just enough fabric, if any, to soften the edges. For others, I add an abundance of fabric if it's appropriate for the rest of the room. Sometimes, 2-inch wooden blinds may be the perfect solution for controlling light while still emphasizing the architectural feature.

## CHOOSE YOUR FAVORITE TREATMENT

Choosing the right window treatment for a room is a big decision. I always start by asking these questions:

- What is your overall style preference?
- Are you formal, fancy, or fresh and simple?

- Does your room have strong architectural features? Are you Romantic or Contemporary in style preference?
- How much light do you like in your rooms?

I like a lot of light, so sheers work perfectly for me. A new idea for those of you with large expanses of glass walls is an innovative system of panels that move laterally on a track. They are simple and sophisticated and create a stunning effect. You can find them at Smith & Noble (www.smithandnoble.com).

Do you have antiques or artwork that need to be protected from UV rays? For many of my clients I have a sunshield coating applied to windows to keep harmful sun rays away. In fact, it often lowers air-conditioning costs as well. Another option is solar shades. They diffuse

light and UV rays while managing glare on TVs and computer screens. But these don't work with every style of décor and can be clumsy.

Do you need privacy? Do you need a completely dark room for sleeping? For privacy, one of the simplest solutions is bottom-up shades. These shades allow you to cover just the bottom of the window while leaving the top part open to allow natural light into the room. Virtually every window shade—whether cellular, woven, or sheer—offers this option. For those who need absolute dark for sleeping, consider blackout shades. Most shades today have a blackout lining option.

Is there a beautiful view that you would like framed or is there something that you would like to hide outside your window? If it's the view you're looking for, I would suggest a window treatment that starts at the edge of the window trim and extends beyond onto the wall to soften the space, giving the window and the view a beautiful balance with fabric. If you want to hide an ugly view, then use layers of fabrics. An opaque sheer beneath a beautiful pair of side panels will allow light to enter while camouflaging the view.

**BELOW** The padded, upholstered large-scale country check pattern of the valance adds detail and soft styling to this comfortable Transitional kitchen window treatment. (Photographer: Patty Minnick; room courtesy of Charter Homes and Neighborhoods, Lancaster, Penn.)

**OPPOSITE** The large-scale pattern and white background of this window treatment fabric keeps the room simple and uncluttered while adding just enough softening and color for the perfect adornment. (Photographer: Patty Minnick; room courtesy of Charter Homes and Neighborhoods, Lancaster, Penn.)

Will children be using the room? If so, make sure your choices are practical and easy to care for. Start with safety. Pull cords are not recommended for use around children. Children's rooms are very busy places, so you need a durable window covering that is safe and easy to operate. Consider washable fabrics in a simple style.

## CHOOSE YOUR PRICE

Of course, I always discuss costs. Window treatments can be expensive. In fact, how much you want to spend may be your most important consideration. The range of prices is incredible. I often start with the basic needs such as light control and privacy. Then slowly, as budget allows, I tackle each individual room by importance.

When it comes to shopping for window treatments, you have several good choices: catalogs, online stores, home centers, department stores, and interior design and window treatment specialty stores. Where do you begin? It depends on how handy you are and how much time you are willing to devote to a project.

## GET ACCURATE MEASUREMENTS

The key issue for all window treatments is to measure properly. Both shades and blinds can be mounted either inside or outside the window casing. You will need to consider the depth of the window casing if you opt for an inside mount. If the casing is too shallow, your blinds might jut out farther than the casing. Outside mounts should cover the entire window. You can choose to hang rods directly onto the casing or a few inches above. If you opt for above, you will need to add a projecting spacer so that your blind doesn't get caught on the top casing.

Measuring for draperies gets more complicated as the window treatment gets more elab-

orate. If you are simply looking for side panels, it's a relatively easy project. Using a metal tape measure for accuracy, determine how high you want to mount your rod and measure down to the floor. Then add 4 to 12 inches of extra length if you want your fabric to puddle on the floor. You will also need to know how many widths of fabric you want for each panel. Generally speaking, a standard 54-inch-wide fabric will pleat down to about 18 to 20 inches in width. For simple side panels that will be used to soften the edges of your window and will not open or close, I generally use at least 1½ widths of 54-inch fabric. If it's silk fabric, I use

2 widths. If you want traversing panels that open and close, you will need to measure the width of your window. Then add extra fabric for extending beyond the frame. For example, if you want your draperies to extend 10 inches beyond the frame of your window and your window is 70 inches wide, then you would add 20 more inches, 10 for each side. This total number (90 inches) now must be multiplied by how much fullness you prefer. For traversing draperies, I prefer two times fullness. Therefore, I would multiply 90 inches by 2, which equals 180 inches. To this, I still need to add fabric for side hems and returns. A return is the distance from the front of your drapery rod back to the wall. In most cases, this is about 3 or 4 inches. Let's assume 4 inches. You will therefore need 8 inches (a return on each side of the window) and you will need approximately 12 inches of fabric for double-turned side hems, giving you a total fabric width of 200 inches. If your fabric is a standard 54 inches wide, you would divide 200 inches by 54 which equals 3.70 widths. Hence, you would need to order 4 full widths of fabric.

Some really good Web sites are available for window treatment shopping. Smith & Noble (www.smithandnoble.com) also has a catalog. This company is great for shades and blinds and has more than two hundred different fabrics to choose from for pleated drapery panels. It also has a ton of detail options available as well as hardware. In addition, it has an excellent online "how-to" resource library for measuring, installing, and designing window treatments.

One of my favorite online companies is Silk Trading Company (www.thesilktradingco.com), where you can choose ready-made or custom-styled draperies. I have visited a few of the

**ABOVE** Vibrant colors and circles prevail in this home office, from the concentric circles of the chandelier to the boldly colored drapery panels. The repeating of shapes and colors adds harmony and whimsy in a sophisticated style. (Photographer: Patty Minnick; room courtesy of Charter Homes and Neighborhoods, Lancaster, Penn.)

**OPPOSITE** The few seemingly different items in this arrangement come together to create a beautiful and interesting composition. (Photographer: Lynn Noble; Interior Designer: Gail Dunn)

stores as well. It is a reliable source whose quality is worthy of any home.

If you have doubts about your measuring ability or are not sure about the style of treatment or even fabric selections, then I highly recommend using a professional. You cannot imagine the difference a professional installation makes until you see it. Dressing a drapery fabric is indeed a fine art. The good installers are worth their weight in gold. Now here's the hard part. You will find it nearly impossible to locate a professional installer who is willing to work directly with a consumer. The reason is simple: They are incredibly busy working for interior designers and window specialty companies. I recently called a few just to be sure, and the response was unanimous—too busy! So be aware that unless you purchase your draperies from a designer or window specialty store, you will most likely *not* be able to find an installer who will hang your draperies. This means that if you choose to buy them online or from a catalog or other general retailer, you will have to hang them yourself. (Note that installers and window treatment specialists are two different professionals. An installer physically installs the treatment; a window treatment specialist designs the treatment and supervises the installation.)

Keep in mind that interior designers or window treatment specialists will be able to provide far more options and insight into the possibilities for your room than you can ever imagine on your own. Most importantly, they can help you develop the best strategy for balancing what you want with what you need and can afford. Your windows are an important element. When dressed properly, they can make your room

sing. For most of my clients, window dressing is the last thing to get done. And that is just fine with me because it gives me the opportunity to truly create a treatment that will complement the rest of the furnishings perfectly.

## NOW DO IT YOURSELF

■ **Be brave and move forward to create window treatments that evoke an atmosphere conducive to the way you want to live.** And don't be afraid to ask for help when you get stuck. Interior designers are friendlier than you think!

# STEP 6: The Art of Arranging Accessories

As I mentioned earlier, I believe that the most inspiring rooms start with decluttering. I also believe that the items we display around our homes should tell the story of our lives while expressing a sense of history, joy, and personality. Sadly, too many people find themselves creating a disarray of clutter rather than providing an inspiring accent. The items displayed in a cluttered room may be the same as the ones in a thoughtfully designed environment, but how they are placed in the room determines whether the objects are art or clutter.

Clutter, as a verb, means, "to fill or cover with scattered or disordered things that impede movement or reduce effectiveness." Artfully arranging items makes them significant. However, the art of arranging is indeed a practiced art. There are a few rules to help guide you, but each situation is unique and requires a bit of patience, editing, and study to find just the right formula to give your room your personal imprint.

When it comes to arranging tabletops, think of all the surfaces in your room as mini-stages. The goal will be to dress each one uniquely, yet tie them together to create a cohesive style all around the room. I always look for something that will inspire a unique direction, whether it's a theme, a color, or even a shape. In my kitchen, the accessories were inspired by my love of birds. Large handcrafted bird sculptures and colorful birdhouses give my kitchen its playful personality. Artistic balance is achieved in finding objects whose shapes, colors, or details add interest to the room. My living/family room accessories are inspired by my love of the beach. My seashell and coral collection takes center stage on my mantel and adds the serenity that I crave.

Whenever I work with clients on accessorizing, I first have them clean all their treasured objects and gather them into one space—categorized by style, size, and color. For example, assemble all vases together and divide by size and color. Then I thoughtfully consider each area within the room to determine which is the most prominent spot to display the most important items. Slowly, I begin to place items, one at a time, often trying different items in different spaces until I find just the right balance.

One of the first decisions I make is whether to work symmetrically or asymmetrically. Symmetry always feels more formal. When working toward symmetry, use symmetrical accessories. Balanced arrangements of like-scaled, matching frames and complementary art styles are perfect for symmetrical designs. Remember that color and texture will also affect your composition. The darker the color,

the more visual weight an item will have. Always consider the background that each item will be placed in front of because it will become part of the composition. Never use a small, delicate item against a strong color, because it simply doesn't have enough visual weight to balance the strength of the color.

## FOLLOW THE GEOMETRIC LINES

Next consider your personal style. If you like more rather than less, use a combination of small and large accessories to create a unique style. If you prefer a cleaner, less cluttered style, choose fewer, larger items and give them lots of breathing room by leaving space around each one. Regardless of which look makes you happy, the rule is that a few well-placed objects are attractive. You do not need to fill every surface in a room. Your goal should be to make the objects that you care about the most look important.

To create balance within a tabletop arrangement, start with your largest or tallest item and add items of declining height. Place tall pieces behind shorter ones. Balance vertical elements with horizontal ones. One of the simplest ways to create a balanced arrangement is to follow the shape of a triangle. The diagonal lines create an illusion of more space, which makes the triangle an ideal arrangement for smaller spaces. As you arrange items, choose a specific item as a focal point so that you don't confuse

the eye by drawing equal attention to two items within the arrangement.

Some of the most interesting tabletop arrangements are as simple as placing objects in single file to create a bold silhouette. They can be identical items or not. A collection of similar items, even if they differ in shape and size, can still be balanced by positioning the larger items toward the outside and the smaller ones toward the center. Another simple yet effective method for arranging is to cluster a group of items in the middle of a table. Four or five interesting vases in similar colors and various shapes and sizes can be gathered together to create an appealing display. On a dining table, a group of objects can be far more interesting than a single center-piece. Remember that collections are meaning-less when they are scattered about a home. They become a worthy collection with significant impact when grouped in a dedicated space.

Mantels are always a significant focal point in a room. Your goal in accessorizing a mantel should be to pair elements that are not only important, but compatible with your mantel style. Often the mantel is a work of art in itself. Keeping a strong yet simple design style might be the best approach for a very detailed mantel. A mantel also presents a unique situation where the wall art is absolutely part of the com-position of the arrangement on the mantel's surface. Artwork or mirrors must be chosen as one part of the whole. Your wall accessories should be comparable in style and color with the objects on the mantel so that the finished composition works in harmony.

## HANGING PICTURES

No matter what wall you are decorating, always consider other objects and furniture.

Planning and coordination are the keys to successful artwork displays. Architectural details and wall shapes and sizes must be considered and incorporated into the overall effect. Perhaps that's why so many people struggle to hang artwork, and it seems to be one of those tasks that create tension between couples. I encourage clients to not take the process so seriously—it's just a nail hole, which I point out is really not a deal breaker and is easily fixed if they decide to move the artwork. Recently, I had a client who refused to hang new artwork because she had just had the room painted and didn't want to ruin the paint job! So there she sits with new furniture and blank walls—and a completely unfinished-looking room.

So let me state for the record: Artwork is not a permanent fixture! In fact, I like rearranging items to make rooms look fresh. Sometimes clients want to leave their walls blank, hoping to "someday" find exactly the right piece of art. But in the meantime, they live with unfinished-looking spaces. I inspire them to consider

**OPPOSITE (TOP)** Linear simplicity gives this entryway a classic grandeur as the grandfather clock and floral arrangement echo the strong vertical lines of the stairway. (Photographer: Patty Minnick; Interior Designer: Sharon Hanby-Robie)

**OPPOSITE (BOTTOM)** Even the vertical wall space becomes part of the composition of this creatively accessorized corner. (Photographer: Lynn Noble; Interior Designer: Gail Dunn)

**RIGHT (TOP)** Symmetry is artfully accomplished when you display a series of pieces framed identically and hung with precision. (Illustrator: Patty Minnick)

**RIGHT (BOTTOM)** To create symmetry with freedom, arrange a variety of sizes and shapes, and maintain consistency by choosing frames in the same color and overall proportion. (Illustrator: Patty Minnick)

something inexpensive that looks good until they find that perfect piece. Art on the walls will certainly make a difference to a room.

Artwork, just like a tabletop display, is a matter of personal style. Are you formal, fancy, funny, or daring? Also consider the style of the artwork itself. Often it dictates how it should be hung. Symmetrical arrangements are the simplest to conceive and often the hardest to hang because they require precise measuring.

One of my favorite arrangement styles is to create a compact arrangement of identical frames of four, six, or more pieces hung closely together with equal spacing between them on all sides. A laser level is very helpful in getting the exact placement of each piece. Before taking hammer to nail, lay out the arrangement on the floor working in vertical columns of two or four and horizontal columns of three or five until you have a pleasing balance with the center at eye level. In other words, you want your columns to be either higher than they are wide or equal, such as two vertical columns and three horizontal, or five vertical and five horizontal columns. When working with an uneven number of rows and columns, keep the space

**OPPOSITE** An odd number of frames creates a visually balanced focal point, giving this family room wall dimension, character, and warmth. (Photographer: Patty Minnick; Interior Designer: Sharon Hanby-Robie)

**ABOVE** A simple plate rack becomes a work of art against a dining room wall when properly accessorized. (Photographer: Patty Minnick; room courtesy of Charter Homes and Neighborhoods, Lancaster, Penn.)

between the vertical columns to about 1½ to 2 inches. For the horizontal space, use 4 to 6 inches. When working with an even number of rows and columns, keep the spacing equal, no more than 2 inches apart.

Another interesting way to create symmetry with more freedom is to arrange a variety of sizes and shapes, but maintain consistency by choosing frames in the same color and overall proportion. For example, if you have four black-framed mirrors that are generally shaped like an oval, you can stack two in the center vertically at the center point of your arrangement. Then position the other two mirrors on each side of the stack with their center points horizontally even.

Unusually shaped wall areas can be the most interesting ones to fill. Consider the side of a staircase. By selecting frames in the same color you can unite a variety of interesting subjects such as artwork, mirrors, photos, and framed objects. Then simply tier your display to follow the slope of the staircase and stagger the heights of the frames within each row as you proceed, moving from left to right. You can also vary the space between frames to keep it interesting. When working with photos, never combine black-and-white photos with color photos. It's too distracting.

## CREATE HARMONY IN YOUR DESIGN

Hanging art asymmetrically is a lot like collage work. You connect the grouping with a unifying color or by arranging compatible shapes or subject matter. Sometimes the furniture directs the form for arranging the artwork that you want to hang. One designer covered an entire wall with a daring bit of what some might consider mayhem—he gathered all of his art and covered the wall, from the floor to the ceiling, and included a very ornate antique three-drawer chest as part of the arrangement. He did not center the chest on the wall, but placed it to the left and used bold, large artwork to counterbalance it. The result was surprisingly attractive with lots of color and a unique appearance.

Of course, that designer has had a lot of practice in the art of picture hanging, so for the sake of those who are not quite ready for such a daring feat, let me give you some basic rules to follow. Artwork should be hung so that it appears to have a relationship with the other objects around it. In other words, a painting hanging 24 inches above an object does not relate to anything. It used to be said that artwork should be hung at eye level. However, my

**OPPOSITE** An infusion of color welcomes guests with this Williamsburg style wall covering that incorporates all the colors used within the home, while a few strategically arranged items add interest and balance to a hand-painted cabinet. (Photographer: Lori Stahl; Interior Designer: Sharon Hanby-Robie)

**ABOVE** A simple wall shelf with artfully placed accessories adds depth and style to a Country kitchen. (Photographer: Lori Stahl; Interior Designer: Sharon Hanby-Robie)

husband is 6 feet 4½ inches and I am 5 feet 2 inches. Whose eye level should we use?

Artwork should be hung no more than 8 to 10 inches above an item. In a hallway, hang wall decorations so the midpoint is standing at about 5 to 6 feet from the floor. In a dining room, art should be closer to the seated-eye level. Seated-eye level is about the same for most people—48 to 52 inches above the floor—so place the center of the wall art at this height. It's not a good idea to hang a single painting over a sofa, even if the painting is large—including another element such as a sconce adds interest and texture. The artwork should cover about 75 percent of the width of the furniture below. If your artwork covers less than 75 percent, add other items to embellish the wall. Consider additional artwork, sconces, decorative wall shelves, and candelabras.

Another no-no is hanging two small pieces of art over a sofa. I would much rather see you choose one large-scale painting and then add the two smaller ones to the composition. A group of pictures should be considered a single unit. Your goal should be to arrange them to create a visually interesting and balanced arrangement. When working with a grouping, choose frames carefully. You can mix frames but only if the artwork and artists are different. Stick to one frame style for a series of works.

One of the easiest ways to transfer an arrangement design to your wall is to start with a large piece of craft paper on the floor. Lay out your arrangement on the paper and then trace each frame, then hang the craft paper on the wall and nail through it.

## NOW DO IT YOURSELF

- **Keep rooms fresh by changing tabletop arrangements a few times a year.** Introduce seasonal flowers and objects that reflect your style.

- **Remember, a home is never finished. It should continue to evolve to meet the ever-changing needs of your family and life.** Be not afraid—and enjoy the process!

# AFTERWORD:
# DESIGNING THE HOME YOU LOVE

Good design allows for individuality. The best-designed homes meet the needs of those living there rather than becoming billboards for the architect who created them. A well-designed room should serve as a backdrop for the life you want to live rather than dictating *how* you should live.

And every room should have an element of surprise that makes you smile. Rooms that must be taken too seriously are boring, while rooms that allow a sense of humor will keep you young and relieve your stress. For example, on my mantel I added a sweet little seahorse to a coral and shell arrangement. Each time I look at him, he makes me smile. In my kitchen, the large colorful bird sculptures add the surprise. A well-designed room can allow you to relax and laugh.

A room shouldn't demand a certain response —it should suggest. A living room should suggest that its visitors get comfortable and spend time there. It should suggest that people engage in conversation—which can be

**BELOW** The arrangement of furniture encourages conversation in this elegantly understated family room. (Photographer: Patty Minnick; room courtesy of Charter Homes and Neighborhoods, Lancaster, Penn.)

accomplished simply by how you arrange the furniture. If seating lines up like soldiers along the wall, no one will be able to comfortably speak to each other. But if groupings of chairs are facing each other, people will naturally talk.

Good design is always simple. It doesn't matter whether you are talking about mathematics, science, art, or an interior of a house; the simple truth is that less is more. For interior design, this means creating beauty that depends on a few carefully chosen elements rather than an onslaught of superficial ornamentation. Creativity is best when it is uncomplicated.

The best design plans begin by focusing on a problem. Form should follow function by solving problems beautifully. The problem will direct the solution and the degree of ornamentation necessary to create a room that is artistic and pleasing to the eye—not overwhelming. If we overdo with lots of pompous embellishments, we create rooms that intimidate, not invite.

Recognize, too, that most of us only change our home furnishings two or three times in a lifetime. The choices you make need to be timeless, bringing together the best of the new with the best of the old. When we aim toward timeless, we avoid the temptation of "fashion." Fashion by definition is always changing, so striving to attain it is futile.

Remember, too, that all interior design must be congruous with the style of the house itself. You cannot ignore the context if you are to create a room that is in good taste. The "taste" or flavor of your style should also reflect the region where your home is located. Every decision you make should be filtered through the architectural and regional context of your home.

Good taste reflects the personality and spirit of the individuals residing in a home. It is something that gives life a sense of quality while <u>delighting the senses</u>. Without good taste we would find rooms functional but not inspiring.

I want to create interiors that delight. I want you to have the freedom to make choices that make sense for you and your family and the way you want to live. I refuse to create spaces that dictate life. <u>Life should dictate design</u>. It doesn't matter how much money or status you have—the environment in which you live can enhance the quality of your life.

I think the complexity of a well-composed space with its textures, temperaments, and visual effects can only be achieved when you make a commitment to balancing the necessary tools for daily living with something beyond the ordinary. As you think about decorating your home, let your personal experiences guide your sense of style. <u>Your home should tell the story of your life</u>. Sometimes that means including an old painting that was your grandfather's favorite. Other times, it means accepting the fact that your grandmother's old bed simply doesn't fit your sense of taste, no matter how you dress it. <u>Be honest, creative, and selective, and you will enjoy good style</u>.

In closing, let me encourage you. This is your home—an environment you control. It should be a place that enhances the quality of your life and your relationships. Live in it and love in it. Let it be the place for good memories and a fulfilling life.

# INDEX

# ABOUT THE AUTHOR

**Sharon Hanby-Robie** is an interior designer and an Allied member of the American Society of Interior Designers. She is the resident home-décor expert and on-air personality at QVC, Inc. She is the author of several books, including *My Name Isn't Martha, But I Can Renovate My Home*. She lives in Lancaster, Pennsylvania.